INSIDE A
THUG'S HEART

ANGELA ARDIS

INSIDE A THUG'S HEART

With original poems
and letters by

TUPAC SHAKUR

Dafina Books

KENSINGTON PUBLISHING CORP.
http://www.kensingtonbooks.com

DAFINA BOOKS are published by

Kensington Publishing Corp.
119 West 40th Street
New York, NY 10018

All Kensington titles, imprints and distributed lines are available at special quantity discounts for bulk purchases for sales promotion, premiums, fund-raising, educational or institutional use.

Special book excerpts or customized printings can also be created to fit specific needs. For details, write or phone the office of the Kensington Special Sales Manager: Kensington Publishing Corp., 119 West 40th Street, New York, NY 10018, Attn. Special Sales Department. Phone: 1-800-221-2647.

Dafina Books and the Dafina logo Reg. U.S. Pat. & TM Off.

ISBN-13: 978-1-4967-1867-9
ISBN-10: 1-4967-1867-4

First Hardcover Printing: May 2004
First Trade Paperback Printing: August 2009

10 9 8 7 6 5 4 3

Printed in the United States of America

This book is dedicated to the memory of
Tupac Amaru Shakur
"Thank you."

And to the memory of my father
Lawrence Ardis
"I love you, Daddy."

Acknowledgments

To Afeni Shakur, thank you for allowing this book to see the light of day. Your blessings and support during this process will have me forever grateful to you. I hope you feel I've done well by Tupac.

To my mother, thank you does not begin to convey the gratitude I hold for you. But since I can't think of a stronger word, thank you will have to do. Thank you for always being by my side. You are the rock that has never faltered, the wind beneath my wings and the air that I breathe. You're the reason I'm here, the reason I've sustained and the reason I remain. Your words and everlasting presence has made me the woman that I am today. Thank you!

To my agent, Alex Smithline, thank you for your patience and endurance.

To my attorney, David Byrnes, you have been so incredible and supportive through this entire process. Thank you. We have so many more projects to go. I hope you're ready!

To my editor, Karen Thomas, thank you for having the vision and insight to see this book as the blessing it was truly meant to be. Considering we're both

Geminis, it's a wonder we were ever able to have a solid conversation. However, with the one hundred people we represented on the phone, I think we did pretty damn good! I believe we'll have a relationship that will last for many years to come.

To Karolyn Ali, thank you for having such patience while reading this book. I feel like we grew closer every day and you, too, were able to see and feel the connection that was made on these pages. I know we will be friends for many years to come. Thank you!

To my business partner, Cedric Pendleton, thank you! For all the arguments, disagreements, frustrations, and conversations . . . here it is! Fruition! Your strength, persistence and "know-how" got us from conversation to reality. Thank you for always lending me an ear and your undivided attention when I needed someone to talk to, to vent to, or to cry to. You never turned me away and I have mad, crazy, stupid love for the man that you are and the life-long friend that you will be. Now let's get crackin' on the next project!

To my business partner, Mike Waller, thank you for having the courage to step up that day at Interscope. God puts people in your life for a reason, a season, or a lifetime. Your presence in my life has its definite reasons, and I know you will remain there for the rest of my life. Your ideas never cease to amaze me, and your patience in explaining everything to me so that I, too, can have the knowledge is one of many of the greatest gifts you could ever have bestowed upon me. Knowledge is power! We have so much more work to do. Don't forget the champagne in the penthouse! See you there!

To my sister, Renee, thank you for always being my cheerleader for anything I ever decided to do. You've always believed in my abilities even when I didn't. Your constant optimism created strengths in me that helped me overcome so many obstacles in my life. "If You Believe" is my anthem thanks to you. Every time my inner child gets scared, I call you and you have a way of injecting that child with such confidence, that we now believe we can do almost anything. Thank you for being a wonderful sister and my best friend.

To my brother, Eddie (Henry, as most know him), my ace, the number one man in my life. Even though you are my brother, you have been like a father to me as well. I measure every man that comes into my life against you, and considering I'm single, this means none of the knuckleheads have measured up. Thank you so much for always giving me business advice and advice about love from a "mature man's" perspective. Thank you for having my back, no matter what, and for being such a strong black man that I can look at you and know that strong black men with no bullshit really do exist. I maintain hope in finding that because of you. Thank you!

To my niece and nephew, Crystal and E.J., I love you two so much. I know I've been pretty preoccupied with my life for the past few years, but now I'm in a place where I can be the auntie that I used to be.

To my good friend Derrick: man, I don't know how to thank you for everything you've ever done for me over the last fourteen years. You have been such a godsend that words cannot begin to express my level of thankfulness for you. You are the realest as a person, a confidant, and a friend. You are the epitome of what friendship represents, and I am truly blessed that we met and maintained. Thank you!

To one of my closest friends, Tanya, thank you. Even though I didn't like you when I first met you, you have been such an incredible blessing in my life. We have been through some of the most traumatic experiences of our lives together and have shared so many good times, too. Over the last ten years, we have leaned on each other, encouraged each other, motivated and inspired one another. I will always be here for you no matter what, where, when, or what time. You are my dog fo' life! Luv you, girl!

To my closest, boogie, undercover goofy friend, Cheryl, thank you. You, too, have been a major blessing in my life for the last twelve years. We have been through it! No more needs to be said! Thank you for always projecting positiveness when it came to anything I was trying to do. I'm here whenever you need me! Luv you, girl! Stay strong.

To my newest and coolest buddy, Iris, thank you. Girl, all I can say is that we got through it and D.D.P. is still in effect but we are looking at it from the outside. A toast to us and that mess! Didn't think we'd make it out. Thank you for always waking up in the middle of the night to hear me vent. I needed it and I appreciated it even more. I couldn't have gotten through so many things without your unconditional support. It always feels like I'm telling you something for the first time even when I've told you thirty times. I hope I have been and will be as good a friend to you as you have been to me for the last four years. The "pipes" are officially down, dog! Luv you, girl!

To my friends, Kirven, thank you for letting me chill when I needed to and always playing the music I wanted to hear at the clubs you deejay at. Tell yo' boys I'll come and cook ya'll some more smothered chicken and peach cobbler soon! Charlie, my Puerto Rican chica, you are such a great friend to me and I know we will grow old together, talking shit about you know what. Everything is going to work out, girl, and if you ever need anything, you call me! We have business to handle! Alicia, girl, here it is! Can you believe it? Three and a half years later and here is the book on the shelf. You are such a blessing to me. Thank you for being there to crack that whip! I know we'll be friends for life. Dukeum, I've known you for twenty-one years. You know you are my forever friend. I love you, man. Don'nae, even though we only talk once every few years or so, you still are on the top of my list of real friends. When we talk it always feels like we just talked yesterday. I miss you, girl. Dutch, thank you for letting me chill when I needed to. I needed it a lot more than you knew. The Thai food and my magnificently made margaritas made it all good, too! Look forward to doing business with you in 2004. Terrell, nobody would know you are an attorney 'cause you so goofy. You have been a blessing and I know we will be friends for life. Syke, I couldn't believe you were standing in Interscope that afternoon and had just been talking about me a month earlier. I'm glad we ran back into one another and I look forward to doing business with you. Trent, thank you for embracing me on G.P. I know we'll be friends and doing business together for many years to come. Dust off your tennis rackets! Darice, we have so much work to do, girl! I'm glad we connected and I know that we'll be friends for a long time. Donte, thank you for your constant optimism and encouragement. Much luv to you. Teresa, my knowledge guru and spiritual advisor, thank you for never judging me and loving me no matter what. I love you sooooooo much! Jetta, my second mama and close friend. I love you and appreciate everything you've ever done for me. We need to get together again soon and exhale! Sully, you know you have been a rock in my life for many many years and I love and appreciate you to the infinite degree. You da man! Poche, see, I'm the only girl in your life that is just your friend. I told you! We must do In & Out Burgers when I get back to L.A. Steve, you have always had my back since I met you. You just kind of took me under your wing and looked out for me like a sister. I love and appreciate you more than you know. Kofie, my exhale buddy. Thank you for the numerous times you let me chill out at our spot to get away. I always enjoy our conversations and the energy that you possess. We will be friends for life. Can't stop what's supposed to be! Darrell, dog, you have had my back since 1989 and if there is ever anything I can do for you, you just holla! It's all a journey. Vincent, you are a godsend if I'd ever seen one. Thank you does not begin to say enough but I think you know what I'm saying. You are a blessing. Sydney, thank you for whipping this body into shape. Couldn't have done it without your kickboxing and boot camp classes. Travis, my new-found friend, you have brought another level to my life and by the time this book comes out, I'll be interested to see what has taken place! Your energy is magnetic and I love spending time with you. I'm always relaxed when I'm with you. Thank you for your constant optimism when it came to this project or anything I was trying to do. Hope you have a great season! Much love, baby.

To my friends, Michael, Trisha, Donna, Izora, Uncle Lynn, Camilla, Moe, Billy, Kim, Roy, Carl, Terry, Todd, Hugh (Road Dog #1), Tyrone (Road Dog #2), S.S, Lori, Najj, William, Tony, John, Stephanie (thank you so much for everything), Jasmine, Re Re (Margaret), Snowball and Granny, Andrew and Darlene, thank you all for always trying to keep me in a positive frame of mind and for being so supportive.

If I have forgotten anyone, I swear I tried not to, but please forgive me. I thank you, too.

Contents

Chapter 1

THE BET

I t was close to 10 P.M. and the office was pretty empty. However, due to a board meeting scheduled for the following week a core group of us was working to critique our financial reports and presentations, blazin' R & B over the constant and steady rhythm of the copy machine. By 10:30 P.M., we were all exhausted and delirious, when M. C. Lyte's song "Ruffneck" came on the radio. My coworker and roommate, Tanya, and I looked at each other, put our coffee mugs down, turned the radio up, and started dancing.

We danced and chanted.

During our impromptu concert, our other coworkers started dancing. We were all even more exhausted when the song ended, but we were energized, and with perfect timing, our Chinese food finally arrived.

"If you could have a 'ruffneck,' who would you pick?" a coworker asked, swallowing her chow mein.

"Treach, with his chocolate, built, rough self," my roommate blurted out, referring to the Naughty by Nature lead rapper. Laughter echoed throughout the empty office.

"What about you, Ann?" someone asked. (I was sometimes called Ann for short.)

"Treach is fine, but I would pick Tupac," I answered. "Sexy, rough, and gorgeous."

They all laughed. "Yeah, right!"

"'Yeah, right,' what? You asked who I would pick. Tupac," I said, defending myself.

"Well, too bad. He's in jail now," someone said.

"So, I didn't say I would go get with him. I said I would pick him. Why are ya'll bashing me? You didn't say anything when Tanya said Treach."

"Yeah, well. Treach is out and about, and the possibilities are actual possibilities. But Tupac? He's gonna be locked up and out of commission for a while," my coworker shot back, laughing.

"Treach is as much of a possibility as Tupac is, as far as that goes," I said. "Tanya would have to get through his girl's ass kickin', if he even wanted her in the first place!" Everyone laughed. "Besides, Tupac is not beyond reach," I added, knowing that he was.

"He's in jail, Ann. He's beyond reach."

"What does that mean? Jail is not beyond reach," I said matter-of-factly.

"Okay. Well, then I bet you can't reach him," my coworker challenged.

"Reach him?" I questioned. "Yeah, right. I thought we established the fact that he's in jail. I meant that he's not out of reach to everyone. But he is out of reach for me. I don't know him."

"You're the one who said he's not beyond reach. I bet you can't reach him," she said with a laugh, raising her eyebrows.

I imitated her, raising my eyebrows, and leaned into the circle that we had created on the floor. "Bet," I said.

We all laughed at the absurdity of the bet and finished our food, then eventually, somewhere around midnight, we completed the task at hand and went home. Thank God it was Friday.

That night, as I began to fall asleep, I chuckled at the thought of Tupac. I was clueless as to how I would actually reach him. I didn't know anyone who knew him or anybody who knew someone who knew somebody who knew him either. But it was a bet, and even though I try hard to win my bets, I always lose. *Always.* But I was up for the challenge.

Yeah, right! Who was I kidding?

The next morning, I was startled awake by the ringing of my phone. I had been sleeping soundly and was pissed that I hadn't remembered to turn off the ringer. It was a guy I had just started seeing. We were supposed to get together that afternoon, but I told him that I had had a late night. He could hear the tiredness in my voice and told me to call him later. I hung up, flipped onto my back, and gazed around my room. Today was definitely going to be a cleanup day. My perfume, makeup, and hair stuff were spread all over my dresser, and the sun, which played peak-a-boo through the blinds, showed me exactly how badly I needed to clean my mirror. I looked over at the clock and was amazed at the fact that it was 2 P.M. Hearing BET blasting on the TV and smelling the aroma of something special cooking on the other side of my bedroom door, I knew that Tanya was up. I cleaned myself, threw on a robe, and went and sat on the living room couch.

"Tired?" Tanya asked, sitting on the love seat across from me.

"Yeah."

"Mmm mmm," she mumbled, eating a morsel of chicken. "Mmm mmm. You can eat," she said, smacking her lips.

"Okay, I kind of figured that, Tan," I said sarcastically.

"I would have fixed you a plate, but I wasn't sure if you were ready to eat yet," she said, laughing at whatever was on the tube.

"I must have missed it when you asked me," I said, closing my eyes as she looked up from her plate.

"I didn't even know you were up. What's wrong with you? You on your period?" she asked, stank as she can sometimes be.

"Maybe."

"Well, you started early 'cause I'm not on mine yet. Or maybe I'm late," she said, looking like she was racking her brain cells. "Naw, I'm not. Then what's your problem, Sybil?"

"Mood swinging. The moon must be full."

Tanya began flipping through the channels and stopped to watch the end of a Naughty by Nature video. "Girl, there's my picky, snicky Treach!" she yelled, bopping around with her mouth full of food.

"Girrrrrl. That man right there? Whew! The things I would do," she went on.

"I know, girl. I know." I laughed, closing my eyes.

"So, have you figured out your plan yet?" she asked.

"What plan?"

"Your plan of attack for your bet."

"Girl, please. I'm not thinking about that bet."

"That was pretty silly of them to bet you that anyway. Like you could actually reach him."

"Yeah, it was the exhaustion of working late, that's all."

"Do you want to go to the mall?"

"You don't have to ask twice," I said, jumping off the couch and heading for my room. "Just give me a minute to throw on some clothes," I yelled.

"I thought you and What's-his-face were supposed to go out this afternoon."

"We're getting together later."

"Oh, okay. Then let's go."

The craziest things kept happening on the journey to the mall. When we first got in the car, Tanya had a mix tape that started playing Tupac's "Holler If Ya Hear Me." Then when we got to the mall, there was a music store at the entrance that had a huge 2Pac poster on display and was blasting his song "I Get Around." Were these signs? Coincidences? Maybe.

After spending most of Saturday shopping, we got home pretty late. I was hanging up my new stuff when it dawned on me that I should just write him a letter. A simple letter. I know that doesn't sound original, but in a situation like this, who cares? What would be the probability of the letter ever reaching him anyway? The odds were staggering to me. In my mind, the likelihood was very low that he would get it, and the likelihood that he'd read it was even lower. I wondered how many letters he got a day. Thousands, I figured. But then I thought to myself, *What do I have to lose?* I lose bets all the time, so what difference would one more make. Right? Right.

I had read that Tupac was at Rikers Island, and I figured I would call New York and ask for his information. Could it be that easy? I didn't think so. I figured they would give me a hard time because of his celebrity. But guess what? I picked up the phone, called Rikers Island, and got his address and prisoner number in a matter of a few seconds. I remember staring at it for the longest time. I was somewhat dumbfounded at how uncomplicated it had been to get, but also wondered again about the possibilities of him ever reading my letter. Why would he? My letter would be just words on a piece of paper from some girl, sealed in an envelope that would be tossed in a sack with thousands of other envelopes.

"Well, that sounds simple enough," Tanya said, watching me put on my face.

"It seems almost too simple. I'm sure he gets lots of letters, and who am I?" I questioned.

"Yeah, I know. He probably just looks for the familiar and is like 'whatever' with the rest," she responded.

"That's what I'm thinking, too. But, you know, sometimes the most obvious is the least difficult. I guess I always think things have to be more complicated."

The doorbell rang.

"Being that it's Tupac, I guess you would think 'complicated' is the operative word," Tanya said. "I guess you're gone for the night," she said with a smirk, referring to the doorbell, which rang again.

"Nope. I'll definitely be back."

"How do you know?"

"Because tonight, I'm not in the mood for anything else," I said, walking past her.

Tanya laughed and headed for her room as I greeted my date and immediately left the house.

I got up Sunday morning filled with an idea. Sometime during the night, my mind had begun trying to figure out how I could make my letter stand out from the rest. When I opened my eyes, the first thing that came to my mind was to use a different color envelope. That would make it stand out from the other envelopes. I threw my down comforter back, handled my business in the bathroom, selected my black Nike sweat suit, and headed towards the door to go to Kinko's.

"Where you goin'?" Tanya startled me, seeming to appear from nowhere. "I'm sorry. Did I scare you?" She laughed.

I caught my breath and picked up my purse off the floor. "I'm going to Kinko's. Why aren't you at church?"

"I'm having TV service this morning."

"Well, I'm off. Be back soon," I said, and I was out the door.

Kinko's was pretty crowded, and finding a parking space was a fiasco in itself. I found my way to the envelopes and admired the array of options. There were so many colors: several shades of red, orange, and yellow; a few different greens; and numerous blues and purples. It looked like a Crayola box had collided with an envelope box. After spending an hour scanning the colors, and thinking about the color ink I would use to address the envelope and whether it would read well or be too much, I chose fuchsia. Yup, fuchsia. I spent another thirty minutes in the cashier's line and came out with one fuchsia envelope. I had also thought about typing the letter on fuchsia paper, but decided that would make the letter too hard to read no matter what kind of ink I used. I was so pleased with my purchase and thought I was so brilliant, as if no one else in the world would think to send a different color envelope. I was convinced that no one else would. I raced home to compose my letter.

Dear Tupac,

My name is Angela, and I am writing you this letter, not as a groupie, but just as a black female who thinks there is more to you than what the media portrays. I saw an interview you did, and I could feel your energy. I don't know about the other incidents, but I think you got a bad rap this time. I have my own views, as does everyone else, but as far as you are concerned, in my eyes, justice was not served. What I've heard about you in the press I'm sure has its truths, and only you know how much of it you are responsible for. But I think you have so much talent and so many gifts that if any of the truths are yours alone, you should assess them and find out why they are in your life and what good, if any, they are doing you as a person. However, I did not write you to lecture you because you're a grown man. I just want to express my thoughts to you and tell you to keep your head up because there is someone out here who believes in the person behind your eyes.

Just a bit about myself, in case you choose to write back. I'm 24, living in Atlanta, Georgia and I work as a marketing assistant, as well as a model. I just ended a five-year relationship and now have a roommate. I'm breathing again for the first time in a long time. Enjoying life. I don't want you to think that I want anything from you because I don't. I'm sure you have enough people around you who want, need, and desire things of and from you.

I'm going to give you my phone number, if you should decide to call. I work 9 to 5 and am home normally by around 6 P.M. Feel free to write to me at the address on the envelope. If you choose to do neither, that's fine, too. Just remember that there is a lesson in your situation. Find it, address it, absorb it, and release the resentment. It will only cause your soul to decay. You are a gift, Tupac. But you have to believe it, too.

Keep Your Head Up,
Angela

The letter took me ten minutes to write.

"What do you think?" I asked Tan.

"It's you."

"What does that mean?"

"It's very direct and to the point."

"Oh. Should I add anything else? Maybe send a picture?" I asked, unsure.

"Naw, just send it," she replied. Then she changed her mind. "Well, yeah. Send a picture." She smiled.

"You think? I figure if he's going to respond at all, I just kind of want it to be because of what I wrote."

"Well, you're trying to win a bet, so if enclosing a picture helps, then hey, stick a picture in. Definitely send a picture." We laughed.

"That boy is used to beautiful women, and I'm not prettier than anything he's ever seen before."

"Ann, jus pit a picture in it," she said in her most exaggerated country accent and winked. "Don't worry 'bout the rest."

I lay in my bed, anxiously staring at the address and prisoner number. What was I doing? What did I think was going to happen? I tossed around a few possibilities in my head, but didn't really believe any of them for a minute. Putting the address on my nightstand, I turned the light out and took a deep breath. It was kind of late and I had to be at work in the morning, but I was restless, wired, and unsettled. I needed to relax and go to sleep. A mental distraction that would put me to sleep was a necessity tonight. I thought of calling Tanya and just talking to her until I fell asleep, which was something we did often, but that didn't tickle my fancy. So I called the guy I had been seeing. He came over and distracted me enough to allow me to finally fall asleep.

I got to work early and typed up the letter on my computer. The office was tranquil and silent as I sat there staring at the words on the screen. My roster of potential scenarios was getting longer and longer every time I thought of my letter being in his hand or in the bottom of a bag. I didn't know which of the scenarios made me feel more comfortable. I knew, in my heart, what would probably happen. But I'm a dreamer, and there is nothing wrong with that.

Another bet down the drain, I thought to myself. The cursor blinked at the bottom of the page to the beat of my heart.

"What are you doing?" I whispered. "What am I doing?"

I must have sat there for a good thirty minutes because when I came to, my coworkers were arriving. I printed out the letter and went to join the coffee crew. At lunch, I raced home, read the letter again, and sprayed it with my signature perfume, Perry Ellis 360°. I inserted a simple picture of my face, sealed the envelope, addressed it, sprayed it again, and scurried to the post office. I had forgotten that I didn't have to address the actual envelope, considering I was going to send it by overnight mail, but I wanted to make sure that there would be nothing to deter my letter from at least making it to Tupac's bag of mail. I had just finished filling out the Express Mail paperwork when the postal worker yelled out, "Next!"

"You smell great," the postal worker said with a smile. "What can I do for you today?"

I placed the Express Mail envelope on the counter, and from my purse I pulled out my fuchsia envelope.

"Now, that's an envelope," the postal worker said with a chuckle. I took it as a sign that I had at least made the right decision color-wise.

"Thank you. I need to send this 'next day.'" I smiled and put the fuchsia envelope inside the Express Mail envelope and gave it to him.

"Someone must be very special to get such beautiful smells sent their way." At that moment, he looked at the address, then back at me, and back at the envelope again as he typed the information into his computer. "This should arrive at Rikers by twelve noon to-morrow."

The words, "twelve noon tomorrow" rang in my ears as I stood and watched the postal worker rip off my copy of the form. In the distance, I could hear him explaining how to track the letter to make sure it did get there by noon tomorrow.

"Noon tomorrow," I whispered.

"Yes, noon tomorrow," he said with an odd tone. I came to and realized he was giving me a "I-don't-believe-you-wrote-Tupac-a-letter" look, and I gave him a look back that said, "yes-I-did-and-what-of-it?" I said, "Thank you," and exited the post office.

The warm Georgia air hit my face and I smiled, took a deep breath, and raced back to work.

My letter was on its way.

Chapter 2

THE CALL

For the next couple of days, I didn't tell anyone at the office what I had done. It was my little secret.

A few days later I got home at 2 A.M., and I could see the flashing light from my answering machine. After washing my face, I pressed "Play," and the tape began to rewind as I undressed.

Beep. "Message sent at seven P.M.," my machine announced.

"Hi, honey. It's Mom. It's about seven P.M., and I thought you'd be home by now. Just wanted to chat. Call me when you get in. Love you. Bye."

Beep. "Message sent at eight twenty-four P.M."

"Wha's up? It's Daryl. Where you at? Call me."

Beep. "Message sent at eight-thirty P.M."

"Hi, Angela. This is Tupac. I got your letter today and thought I'd call, but I guess you're not there. I'll try again tomorrow. Bye."

I was frozen in my tracks. I couldn't move.

"He got my letter, he read it, he responded," I whispered. "No, he didn't just respond, *he called!*"

I tried to rewind the answering machine tape to hear the message again, but the machine was old and, of course, on this particular night it decided not to cooperate with me. I flew out of my bedroom and ran like a madwoman to Tan's room.

"Tanya!" I screamed, banging on her door. I didn't know if she had company or was just sleeping soundly. "Tanya!" I yelled again, banging a few more times as I tried to get my arm back through my shirt.

"What? Come in! What's wrong?" she asked, half asleep, half alarmed.

"*He called!*" I screeched.

"Who called?"

"Guess!"

"Ann, it's two o'clock—no, two-seventeen—in the damn morning. Who?"

"Tupac."

"*No!*"

"*Yes!*"

"What did he say?" she asked, sitting up.

"I want you to hear it, but I can't get the tape to rewind in my answering machine. I need you to come with me to the office so that I can get the small recorder."

In the darkness, I heard a very deep breath and a few grunts.

"Why can't you just wait till you get to work tomorrow?" she whined.

"Because I want to hear it again now. Come on! You don't have to go in. Just ride with me."

"Ann, nooooooo," she whined.

She knew me so well. My behavior is sometimes extremely off the wall, and this request didn't surprise her at all. She was just sleepy.

"Tan, you don't even have to get dressed. Just bring your pillow and come on."

I flipped on the light and heard her cursing me out as I ran back

to my bedroom to get the tape and my keys. We lived only five minutes from work, so it wasn't far at all. But it was too dangerous for
her to sit in the car, and once there, the dimly lit parking lot and
hovering shadows convinced her of just that. Even though this was
considered a safe area, we knew that no area was that safe.

"We're going to get arrested," she said, yawning. I checked
around the dark parking lot for moving shadows, but all was still.

"We work here and have keys to the building. Why would we get
arrested?"

"Because we're black, we're in our pajamas, it's two-thirty in the
damn morning, and I'm sure they would believe we were coming
up here to get a tape recorder because Tupac called and your answering machine wouldn't rewind," she said sarcastically.

"Shut up, scary, and come on," I said, entering the building
with her right behind me.

I didn't know where the small recorder was, so I had to look for
it. I started in the back room and worked my way to the reception-
ist's desk. Tanya looked in the conference room and worked her
way to her desk, where I found her half asleep.

"I can't find it," I groaned, sitting in the doorway of her cubicle.

"I don't know where it could be," she mumbled sleepily. "Well,
what did he say?"

I recited the brief message and took a deep breath. Disappointed,
we headed home.

"Well, he said he'd call you tomorrow," she said.

"Yeah, he did."

"What did he sound like?"

"Like Tupac."

"Well, that was a fast response. He must have liked the letter."
She looked at me. "What's wrong? You scared?" she asked, grin-
ning. "Don't trip now. You won the bet. I can't believe he called."

It was now somewhere around 3:30 A.M. We rode the rest of the
way home in silence.

The next day at work, I couldn't concentrate. The buzz was around the office, and no one could believe he had called. If Tan hadn't backed me up about him calling, no one would have believed me. I still couldn't believe it.

"Are you trying to figure out what you're going to say to him?"

"Naw, not really. Just more-so wondering what he's going to say."

I had pretty much wasted an entire day, watching the cursor blink, drinking coffee, and daydreaming about things I knew were as farfetched as what was occurring. *I should have bought a new answering machine in case I miss his call again,* I thought to myself.

"I cancelled my date tonight," I said to Tanya.

"You should have. It's not every day that you get a call from Tupac," she said with a smirk.

"He was upset and wanted to know what happened," I said, referring to my date.

"Did you tell him?"

"Nope! It wasn't his business what happened. All he needed to know was that our plans weren't happening." We started laughing. "Questioning me. Is he crazy? He's not my man."

I had a little something extraordinary going on at the moment, but in all honesty, I really did like the guy I had been going out with. However, my mind wouldn't allow me to get caught up in the reality of a date that evening because I was trying to get a grasp on the bizarreness of a phone call from Tupac. I hadn't thought for one second that he would ever call, and as far as I was concerned, from this moment on, anything was possible.

The day finally ended. I went straight home. I hit the play button on my answering machine and held my breath as the messages played one by one.

Beep. "Message sent at ten A.M."

"Hey, Ang. This is Hugh Dog. Just wanted to see if you and Tan are down for a road trip this weekend. Destination: step show in Florida. Hit me up when you get this. Peace."

Beep. "Message sent at two P.M."

"Hey, it's me. I didn't mean to come off like I was checking on you, but I had bought some tickets to a play tonight and was a little upset that our plans got canceled. Sorry if I upset you. Call me later."

Beep. "Message sent at four forty-seven P.M."

"It's your brother. Call me."

Beep. "Message sent at four fifty-eight P.M."

The caller hung up.

"Damn!" I said. I stood there and wondered if that had been Tupac, not leaving a message this time.

"Did he call?" Tanya knocked lightly on my door, then let herself in.

"I don't know."

"What do you mean you don't know?"

"I got this message around five, but whoever it was hung up."

"It could have been him, huh?" Tanya said, looking in my closet.

"Well, I hope not. I told him that I normally get home around 6 P.M., so maybe it wasn't him."

"Maybe not. Wonder when he will call," she said, walking out of my room with one of my shirts.

"Me, too."

I turned the water on for a shower. I brought the cordless phone into the bathroom, just in case. You can never be too careful. I laughed at myself. I felt like I was in high school again, waiting for some guy to call. I was tripping. Yup, I was definitely tripping. I finished my shower and decided to watch a little pretend television—meaning, I pretended to watch it, while truly trying to keep my mind off the obvious. The silly part about the entire scenario was that Tanya had left and I was home alone and was trying to fool only myself. My phone rang several times, and yes, I jumped at every one of the calls.

I talked to my mom. I argued with my friend because he couldn't understand why I'd canceled our date if all I was doing was watching television alone. Needless to say, he took it personally. I understood, but I just wasn't extremely sympathetic. I talked to another friend of mine, and, of course, Tanya called several times to inquire about the status of my incoming calls. Somewhere close to 9 P.M., I had pretty much given up on the idea that Tupac would call again. I had simply missed my opportunity to chat with him. Wow! What a disappointing moment. But on the brighter side of the situation, I had finally won a bet!

     My phone rang at 9:12 P.M.

"Hello," I said dryly.

"May I speak to Angela?" The voice vibrated through the phone.

"This is Angela," I said, my heart racing a mile a minute. I didn't want to make any assumptions, but I was making one large assumption. No, I was definitely assuming.

"This is Tupac," the caller said, then hesitated.

I thought I was going to fall over. This was crazy. I had just entered the Crazy Zone. "Hey. How're you doing?" I said, trying to lower my heart rate quietly.

"Under the circumstances, fine."

"I heard that." We both laughed nervously.

"I really liked your letter and picture. You're beautiful," he said.

"Thank you. I wasn't sure you would respond."

"I had to. The letter was real, the picture is beautiful, and it smelled so good. I had to call." We laughed.

"I'm glad you did."

"Now I have a sweet voice and laugh to put with everything else," he said, his tone softening.

Is he flirting with me? *I thought to myself.* Nawww. Wishful thinking.

"How did you call me? You have special privileges?" I asked jokingly.

"Yeah, right now I do, but they're gonna ship me outta here soon. I just don't know when."

"How long do you have?"

"One and a half to four and a half years."

"Damn!" I said.

Tanya walked into the house at that moment, talking about I-don't-know-what, and I frantically waved to her to shut up. Excitedly, she mouthed, "Is that Tupac?" and I nodded my head yeah, putting my finger over my mouth.

"Yeah, I know, right? Is it okay if I write you?" he asked, unsure.

"Please do," I said, trying to mask my utter disbelief in what was going on.

"Maybe if we get cool enough, you can come and visit me," he said, hesitating.

I paused briefly. I was surprised that he was even having this thought. I walked briskly to my room, taking the cordless with me, and looked in the mirror. Yes, I was awake.

"Yeah, I'm sure that could be arranged when the time comes," I said quietly, with a smile and a wink to myself in the mirror.

"You bullshittin' me," he said, laughing.

"No, I'm not. I'm serious. Once we get to know each other better, I'd come."

"You'd come? You promise?" he asked.

He wants me to make him a promise, *I thought.* This, I'm sure, was normal for him, now, so I played along. As if things would ever get that far.

"Yes, when that time comes, I promise," I said to him, and we both laughed.

"You gotta keep sayin' 'when the time comes,' right?" he said, chuckling.

"Yeahhhhhhh. Gotta keep sayin' it," I answered, and we laughed again.

"God, you sound sweet," he said with what I imagined to be a smile.

"Thank you." He was flirting with me, I convinced myself.

"Well, they're waving me off the phone, but look for my letter soon, and write me back, okay?"

"Okay."

"Sweet dreams," he whispered.

"Sweet dreams."

"Bye."

"Bye."

"Look!" I said, excited. Tanya turned around and noticed the huge diamond on my finger. Her eyes sprung out of her head.

"Oh my God!" she screamed. "He asked you to marry him?" She jumped up and down.

"Yes! Yes! Yes! Yes!" I screamed, as thoughts of home life and kids ran through my head. So vivid, yet faded by the cloudy atmosphere that dreams create. I could see him standing there in his black tux, made to order like only Tupac can wear: baggy, but tailored. The bridesmaids and groomsmen standing in a row, waiting for me to come through the gated yard. "If This World Were Mine" by Luther Vandross was keyed up, and I appeared at the gate. One hundred doves were released as the white gates opened. Everyone remained standing as I started my walk down the aisle, with white chiffon flowing freely from my

gown, as the wind off the ocean blew its blessings my way. Tupac smiled and looked up to the sky, appreciating the white rose petals that were falling from the heavens. The setting sun bounced off the beads of my gown, illuminating my presence in the aisle as I reached Pac at the altar. He took my hand in his, and a tear fell slowly down my face. Wiping it away, he took my chin in his hand.

"I love you," he said softly.

"I love you, too."

The minister went through the ceremony as the sun went down on the water that formed our backdrop. The blackness was brightened by the appearance of a thousand stars in the sky. After everyone looked in awe at the stars, Tupac and I gazed into each other's eyes with adoration. The minister turned to us and said, "I now pronounce you man and wife." We smiled at each other. "You may kiss the bride," the minister said and closed his Bible as we put our arms around each other and . . .

"If you'd like to make a call, please hang up and try your call again . . . message three-four-two-one-seven." *Beep.* I could hear the operator from a distance. I had not hung up the phone, and the operator had rudely interrupted my train of thought, right at the kiss. I hung up and ran into the kitchen, where Tanya was eagerly waiting with ice cream.

"What? What? What?" She jumped, excitedly shoving a bowl of chocolate ice cream at me and pushing me into the living room. She took her normal spot on the love seat, and I took mine on the couch.

"This is crazy!" I screamed, giving her a "what's-going-on?" look.

"What happened?"

"This is crazy, crazy, crazy!" I screamed.

"Ann, okay, this is crazy. Now what did he say? Before I throw my ice cream at you," she said, with a spoonful of butter pecan pointed in my direction.

"He asked me if he could write me and if, after we get to know each other better, I'd promise to come and visit him."

"He said that?"

"Yes, girl."

"When is he going to write you?"

"I don't know. He just said soon."

I lay in my bed that night and prided myself on the letter, the picture, the perfume, the envelope, the Express Mail delivery, and my spirit to take on and execute the bet. Something within this list of pride-bearing items inspired, triggered, intrigued, or just simply motivated Tupac to call and respond. I didn't know which it was, but I was pleased that he had. No, I was thrilled that he had. It didn't matter to me how many other letters he responded to or how many other females he asked to promise a visit. The only thing that interested me was the fact that he had responded to my letter and had called me—twice—to talk. If this wound up being the extent of our association, I would be fine with it, and I would take what happened as confirmation that the impossible is possible and that probability is just as much a reality as surreal experiences.

But guess what? It was only the beginning.

Chapter 3

THE FIRST LETTER EXCHANGE

t's funny how once something comes into your life or you take notice of something, you begin to repeatedly see or hear things that refer to that something. All of a sudden, I took notice of any- and everything that had to do with Tupac. I wasn't fixated on him, but I constantly noticed reminders of him. For example, I was driving down Cambelton Road and I saw a poster advertising the upcoming re- lease of his CD. I was in the mall and I noticed that his songs were playing. Or I listened to the radio or watched television and took notice when he was being talked about, when before I would have over- looked it and not paid any attention. It happened that day Tanya and I went to the mall before I actu- ally wrote the first letter to him. I know they didn't just start playing his music or hanging his posters— I just started noticing.

My mom wasn't surprised by the series of events, but she was very concerned about the whole situa- tion. She began by asking if I could afford the collect calls. I assured her that he didn't call me collect and ended the conversation by saying this was probably the beginning of the end.

"Angela, please," she responded. She calls me Angela only when she's irritated or angry. I decided she was irritated because this tone usually meant she wasn't going to share her total feelings at this time. I immediately changed the subject.

A beautiful, moisture-filled day encouraged me to walk out and get our mail. As I reached into the box, the sky opened up, and I hurried back to the apartment as a clap of thunder echoed. I flipped through the mail and my eyes read, "Ms. Angela Lovely." I couldn't stop smiling.

SHAKUR 700-94-00110
500 Hazen St. N.I.C. D3
East Elmhurst, N.Y. 11370

Ms. Angela Lovely
1404 Summit Springs Drive
Dunwoody, GA. 30350

Sorry I don't have
Any beautiful
smells
to pass on to you
but Know that
I'm smiling &
considering where
I'm at
That's a plus!

"I just talked 2 you
& you sound
Very Sweet!"

Angela,

You'll have 2 forgive my sloppy handwriting but I don't have the typing skills or the typewriter 2 do this in the neat manner that you did but hey! it's the thought that counts right? ☺ Okay, now how do I begin? First of all I was very impressed with your letter. I have received Many letters since this "incident" and yours is definetly one of the ones that stood out. With all the Drama I've been going through it was nice 2 see there was still a true woman out there that didn't have a problem communicating with a man. I truly appreciate the little things a woman does to express herself, like the perfume and the beautiful pictures. As you already know I am currently being held hostage in Rikers Island State Pen! I'll be moved soon to a real penitentiary upstate in a few days but not too far. As far as this whole Sexual Abuse charge, If you knew anything about me and the character that I possess you would know I AM totally innocent! Unfortunately being a "Thug" and talking shit can get a nigga framed in Amerikkka! I've been sentenced 2 1½ - 4½ years but As long as I chill (which I am) I should be out in 96, the early part if I really behave! ☺ When I do get out, however, I'll be sharper, stronger and even hungrier! As you know I was shot 5 times. Twice in the head once in the hand, once in the leg and one very painful shot in the scrotum. The Two shots 2 the head healed As did the hand leg & family jewels"! I was extremely blessed 2 have taken so much lead and still be able to walk, talk & have babies but GOD was with me and here I am! My new Album "Me Against the World" will be out March 14, and I expect great things from it. So while I'm locked down my business will still be handled! It's good 2 hear you are doing good for yourself. I want to say that's too bad about the end of your 5 year relationship but I'm a real and honest person and really I'm glad his loss my gain!

As 4 me I don't really have a woman but honestly I have a special person in my life but we're more friends than anything. In your letter you made it clear that you didn't want anything from me, well once again keeping it real I can't say the same thing. I would love 2 get 2 know you better and 2 see if we can begin a friendship 2gether. I figure if you can be my friend while I'm in here we'll be real cool once I'm released THINK ABOUT IT! Being in Prison I can't promise you much but I can assure you I am honest, straight forward, caring and DEEP. Being a gemini there are several layers & sides 2 my personality and it's just a matter of getting 2 know each other & finding that right mix that'll click ☺ I guess this is enough for now but I am hardly finished get back 2 me. Be a little more personal. Send me some more pictures and keep me in your prayers & thoughts! In fact every night at Midnite (if your still up) Look at the sky find a star & know that I am somewhere doing the same thing thinking Positive Pleasurable thoughts about you Could you do me that favor!? Until Next time!

Eternally
Yourz
Tupac A.S.
"2PAC"

☺

Angela,

You'll have to forgive my sloppy handwriting but I don't have the typing skills or the typewriter to do this in the neat manner that you did but hey! It's the thought that counts right? ☺ Okay, now how do I begin? First of all I was very impressed with your letter. I have received many letters since this "incident" and yours is definitely one of the ones that stood out. With all the drama I've been going through it was nice to see there was still a true woman out there that didn't have a problem communicating with a man. I truly appreciate the little things a woman does to express herself, like the perfume and the beautiful pictures. As you already know I am currently being held hostage in RIKER'S ISLAND STATE PEN! I'll be moved to a real penitentiary upstate in a few days but not too far. As far as this whole sexual abuse charge, if you knew anything about me and the character that I possess, you would know I AM totally innocent! Unfortunately being a "Thug" and talking shit can get a nigga framed in Amerikkka! I've been sentenced to 1½-4½ years but as long as I chill (which I am) I should be out in 96, the early part if I really behave! ☺ When I do get out, however, I'll be sharper, stronger and even hungrier! As you know I was shot five times. Twice in the head once in the hand, once in the leg and one very painful shot in the scrotum. The two shots to the head healed as did the hand and leg and "family jewels"! I was extremely blessed to have taken so much lead and still be able to walk, talk and have babies but GOD was with me and here I am! My new album "Me Against the World" will be out March 14, and I expect great things from it. So while I'm locked down my business will still be handled! It's good to hear you are doing good for yourself. I want to say that's too bad about the end of your five year relationship but I'm a real and honest person and really I'm glad his loss my gain! ☺ As for me I don't really have a woman but honestly I have a special person in my life but we're more friends than anything. In your letter you made it clear that you didn't want anything from me, well once again keeping it real I can't say the same thing. I would love to get to know you better and to see if we can begin a friendship together. I figure if you can be my friend while I'm in here we'll be real cool once I'm released THINK ABOUT IT! Being in prison I can't promise you much but I can assure you I am honest straight forward, caring and DEEP. Being a Gemini there are several layers and sides to my personality and it's just a matter of getting to know each other and finding the right mix that'll click. ☺ I guess this is enough for now but I am hardly finished get back to me. Be a little more personal. Send me some more pictures and keep me in your prayers and thoughts! In fact every night at midnite (if you're still up) look at the sky find a star and know that I am somewhere doing the same thing thinking positive pleasurable thoughts about you. Could you do me that favor!? Until next time!

ETENALLY
YOURZ

Tupac A Shakur (Signature)
"2PAC"

Sorry I don't have any beautiful smells to pass on to you but know that I'm smiling and considering where I'm at that's a plus! "I just talked to you and you sound very sweet!" 2PAC

Tanya and I lounged and read the letter over and over.

The next morning, I felt like I was about to reveal the largest secret in the universe as I walked into the office, letter in hand. I called an emergency meeting and everyone that was present the night of the bet convened in the conference room.

"What's going on?" one of my coworkers asked.

"Patience. Patience, little one," I teased as everyone took a seat.

"Tanya, the lights," I commanded. The room went dark.

In my best English accent, I said, "I'm not here to take up too much of your time. I just have a little something I want to share. I know that this room is filled with a few nonbelievers. A select few who live in a very small box filled with perfect pictures, colored neatly inside the lines. Those of you who believe in the reality of possibility know what it feels like to color outside of the lines that life draws." Everyone chuckled. "For all present, feast your eyes on the reality of possibility." I then flicked on the projector, which flashed the images of Tupac's envelope and letter on the viewing screen. Gasps filled the room.

"For those in-line drawers, this is a lesson that anything is possible. You don't mess up the picture if you color outside the lines. Rather, you create new boundaries for your picture and, in turn, for your life. That concludes this meeting. Feel free to read the letter at your leisure." I laughed and left the room.

I sat and pondered the fact that no one would have thought that it could be that easy. My mother always says, "Things are only as difficult as you make them or think them to be." I was a believer now. Tupac Shakur had written me a letter. To see what would happen next was what kept me racing back to the mailbox.

Chapter 4

TUPAC REACHES OUT

I decided to send Tupac a card before I wrote him a second letter. I wanted something that was motivational, that pertained to his situation, so I chose one that contained one of my favorite poems, "Footprints in the Sand." I was in the midst of composing my second letter when I received another one from him addressed to Ms. Angela Lovely. I wasn't expecting another one that soon. Then I noticed that the address was different. He had been moved.

Tupac Shakur #95A1140

1E23 BOX F

FISHKILL N.Y 12524-0445

Angela Lovely
1404 Summit Springs Drive
Dunwoody, GA. 30350

U.S. POSTAGE
0.32

MAR-?'95
N.Y.

MARCH 2, 1995

Angela,
    I'm glad I got 2 speak 2 u when I did because at 5:00 A.M. the next morning, Just as I predicted, I was moved to a classification facility upstate in the mountains. My movement is restricted to my cell and I am unable to have visitors or use the phone. I am kept in what is called Administration Segregation. They feel as though either I'm a threat 2 this facility or this facility is a threat 2 me. So once again I am forced to adapt 2 a fucked up situation. I sure wish I had one of your letters in here. So that I could stare at your picture & smell the intoxicating aroma of your perfume. Once I left Riker's Island I was stripped of everything; my letters, cloths, etc. So I am currently imagining or remembering what you look & smell like. If you find the time write me & enclose a more personal letter & picture. Hopefully this won't last long I am being as strong as possible and representing 'THUGLife as I believe it should be. The most pain is Knowing I am in here for something I didn't do! Damn that will never go away, the feeling of helplessness and 2 know my own people set me up! That's alright though, with God beside me and a good woman around me 2 love a nigga like he need 2 be loved the world <u>will</u> be mine once again. So I am asking for your affections from all the way in this cell. Send me some love 2 get me through this stormy weather

Passionately,
2PAC
Tupac A.S.

31

March 2, 1995

Angela,

I'm glad I got to speak to you when I did because at 5:00A.M. the next morning, just as predicted, I was moved to a classification facility upstate in the mountains. My movement is restricted to my cell and I am unable to have visitors or use the phone. I am kept in what is called Administrative Segregation. They feel as though either I'm a threat to this facility or this facility is a threat to me. So once again I am forced to adapt to a fucked up situation. I sure wish I had one of your letters in here so that I could stare at your picture and smell the intoxicating aroma of your perfume. Once I left Riker's Island I was stripped of everything; my letters, cloths, etc. So I am currently imagining or remembering what you look and smell like. If you find the time write me and enclose a more personal letter and picture. Hopefully this won't last long I am being as strong as possible and representing THUGLIFE as I believe it should be. The most pain is knowing I am in here for something I didn't do! Damn that will never go away, the feeling of helplessness and to know my own people set me up! That's alright though, with GOD beside me and a good woman around to love a nigga like he need to be loved the world will be mine once again. So I am asking for your affections from all the way in this cell. Send me some love to get me through this stormy weather.

Passionately,
2PAC

Tupac A Shakur
(Signature)

"He wants you to send him some love," Tanya joked in a raspy voice.

"He wants a pen pal," I said, trying to concentrate on composing my second letter to him. "He already has loved ones, who, I'm sure, are sending him mad love."

"Yes, but he's asking for you to send him some along with your affections. Send him some, girl."

"Whatever."

"You know, with your writing skills, you could send him a little somethin'-somethin' to get him through this typhoon," she laughed.

"I could send him a lot of things that could take his mind somewhere else for a minute."

"So, are you?"

"I'll wait and take it slow."

She glanced at me knowingly again.

"He's not even coming at me like that, Tan."

"Umm huh. Well, I definitely want to read those letters when you start writing them. And you will start writing them. Watch what I say," she said, smirking, as she headed out of my room.

Dear Tupac,

I sent you a poem, but I guess you probably didn't get it because I sent it to Rikers Island. You know you're going to be okay. I think this for two reasons: one, you're a Gemini and we Geminis are chameleons that can adapt to anything and any situation, and second, you're a survivor and this situation will not fold you. My mother always told me—and I'm sure you've heard this a million five times—that everything happens for a reason. Maybe that reason isn't evident right now, but one day, hopefully, it will reveal itself. Just know that God has a plan for you.

In your last letter, you asked me to be a little more personal, so here goes. I was born in Detroit, Michigan; raised in Grand Rapids, Michigan; and at 18 moved to Atlanta. Atlanta is wonderful. My original plan was to enroll in Georgia State University's accounting program, but due to procrastinating on completing the paperwork, I had to sit out. A year later, I began studying accounting at DeVry Institue of Technology, and afterwards, I secured a permanent position with a great company. It's a nice job, the people are cool, and I'm happy. This job is "all about the kids," and I think the world should be "all about the kids." Don't you? I've been modeling since I was 7 years old. I think I probably went to every modeling school that Michigan had to offer. Everything I learned wasn't useful, but it served its purpose. I've taken dance classes for 10 years—jazz, modern, and ballet. I've taken singing lessons, karate, sculpting, guitar lessons, flute lessons, and acting classes. I drove my mom crazy.

I recently met someone who seems cool. We're just kicking it. Neither one of us is looking for a relationship, so we're just enjoying each other's company and, of course, exploring the fuck-buddy experience. I live and work with my roommate, who is a very good friend. I'm maintaining myself and my existence with goals to rule the world, or at least to give it a large injection of my perspective. So, that pretty much sums me up in a nutshell. Hang in there, Tupacalac ☺. I hope you like the pictures I've enclosed. We'll, I'm going to end this now, but I will write you again soon.

Forever,
Angela

P.S. Remember midnight!

I couldn't imagine what it feels like to be locked down, with one's movements restricted to a cell. It must be maddening, especially for a Gemini. It's like caging a hummingbird. Hummingbirds fly with such speed. They're always on the go, always moving. The same is true for a Gemini: we need constant movement because our minds never rest. We're always on the go. So, to cage such a spirit is criminal in itself. Part of me felt sorry for him, and part of me felt that there had to be some truth somewhere in the verdict. But where?

There was something about his wanting and pleas that triggered something inside of me. Even though I knew there were people who cared about him and were there for him, he seemed to also be reaching out to me for something. That something was peaking my curiosity when another letter addressed to Ms. Angela Lovely arrived.

I didn't know what to expect from this letter. According to the date, it had passed my letter enroute. He hadn't yet received my last letter or poem. I considered this correspondence a treat. So I took a shower, popped some popcorn, and, as I lay in my bed, took delight in reading it.

Tupac shakur #95A1140
    BOX F   H8E
Downstate Correctional Facility
FISHKILL, N.Y. 12524-0445

Sen-

MID-HUDSON NY 12555 03/07/85 19:51 DCR4

U.S.POSTAGE
0 32

Angela Lovely
1404 Summit Springs Dr.
Dunwoody, GA. 30350

March 6, 1995

Friend
out Not in   P S

Dearest Angela,

It's feels wierd writing 2 u because I don't really know you that well but 2 me it seems a friendship between the two of us started from out of this crazy situation could be real special. So if I'm writing u 2 much or I began 2 get too personal forgive me and let me know and it will all cease. I hope you can appreciate my honesty. I hope u can feel my sincere effort 2 get 2 know you as a friend and see what grows from that. Is this 2 much 2 ask from you? I haven't recieved your 2nd letter but I hope 2 hear from you real soon. I have at least a year to do so in this year Angela allow yourself to drop your inhibitions and come to me through the pages of your letters. Don't just write pleasant polite things Really reach out 4 me. I desire 2 know you like no one else has known you before. I want desperately 2 be your friend not like a male friend but closer like the girlfriend you trust but not in the feminine sense Just in the sense that you can learn 2 trust me. And share your heart the bright spots and the dark spots. the angers and the passion. Can u feel me? or does this just sound like bullshit 2 U? Be honest I know men in general can be real smooth & full of it but I hope by now you c I'm not like that at least In my heart It is not my intention 2 be that way. Even if you and I never do reach "the next level" I feel like I can be an asset to you. I can be

Someone you can confide in and trust. And because of where I am you know it is not based on a physical thing. Here's my proposition. We become intense pen pals for four to six months, and then we began to see each other that is if you don't mind travelling to a correctional facility to see me and then by the time I am released we should have a strong bond between us. I would even wager to say one of the strongest bonds you've ever experienced. I want to know more about you in 1 year than your unfortunate ex-man knew in 5 years. Is that too much? Then by the time I'm free we can determine if it should either stay innocent & platonic or transpire into the physical. What do you think? Am I bugging? I hope not. You know jail make a nigga say some wild shit but 2 me I feel this in my ♡ so I'm just bringing it to you raw like this. it's my attempt 2 show you how serious my intentions are. No promises or gaurantees just hopes & fantasies. It's all on you now . . . . I'm waiting!

Love
Ur H

P.S. Sorry this shit is so sloppy. . .
but hey I was on a role ☺
Send me another picture. full body this time ☺
So I can see what u look like
HEAD 2 TOE

38

(4 Angela)

"4 THOSE NIGHTS WHEN U R ALONE" By Tupac Shakur

I
U ever share your soul with a Stranger
only To realize he was a long lost friend?
Ever Talk 2 A Man like U talk with a Woman
And share what you can't with other men?

II
Can u picture your love being given
2 A criminal stuck in this Hell
Can u promise 2 hold off from Judging him
until the day when you really Know him well

III
Can u close your eyes and imagine
If everything went Right
The power of passion finally Possessed
After all those sleepless nights

IV
I Bet U think I'm gaming you
Just like all the men in your past
Cuz' ALL of them promised u heaven on Earth
But None of them seem 2 Last

(over)

(CONTINUED)

V   AFTER ALL, WHAT CAN 👁. OFFER u ?
     Besides Lonely Nights & Sweet words
     promises of pleasures 2 come
     And Lines you've ALReady Heard

VI   ALL 👁. Can Say is have faith in me
     And in Time maybe you'll come 2 C
     The definition and TRue Meaning
     OF FRiendship can Be discovered in me

                    (written exclusively 4 Angela from Tupac Shakur)

P.S. Angie, this is but
     a Small but Sincere
     token of my
       intentions 4 u
       Hope you like it
       It is the only one of
           it's kind
       That's on everything
              I Love!
           No bullshit!

                                              Love
                                              Tupac Shakur

(P.S. Again)
   what the hell is your
        last name? ☺

40

Dearest Angela,

It feels weird writing 2 u because I don't really know you that well but 2 me it seems a friendship between the two of us started from out of this crazy situation could be real special. So if I'm writing u 2 much or I began 2 get too personal forgive me and let me know and it will all cease. I hope you can appreciate my honesty. I hope u can feel my sincere effort 2 get 2 know you as a friend and see what grows from that. Is this 2 much 2 ask from you? I haven't received your second letter but I hope 2 hear from you real soon. I have at least a year to do so in this year Angela allow yourself to drop your inhibitions and come to me through the pages of your letters. Don't just write pleasant polite things really reach out 4 me. I desire 2 know you like no one else has known you before. I want desperately 2 be your friend like a male friend but closer like the girlfriend you trust but not in the feminine sense just in the sense that you can learn 2 trust me and share your heart the bright spots and the dark spots. The angers and the passion. Can you feel me? or does this just sound like bullshit to you? Be honest. I know men in general can be real smooth & full of it but I hope by now you c I'm not like that at least in my heart it is not my intention 2 be that way. Even if you and I never do reach "the next level" I feel like I can be an asset to you. I can be someone you can confide in and trust. And because of where I am you know it's not based on a physical thing. Here's my proposition. We become <u>intense</u> pen pals for four to six months and then we begin to see each other that is if you don't mind traveling to a correctional facility to see me and then by the time I am released we should have a strong bond between us. I would even wager to say one of the strongest bonds you've ever experienced. I want to know more about you in 1 year than your unfortunate ex-man knew in 5 years. Is that too much? Then by the time I'm free we can determine if it should either stay innocent & platonic or transpire into the physical. What do you think? Am I bugging? I hope not. You know jail make a nigga say some wild shit but to me I feel this in my heart so I'm just bringing it to you raw like this. It's my attempt 2 show you how serious my intentions are. No promises or guarantees just hopes and fantasies. It's all on you now . . .

I'm waiting!

LOVE
2PAC(signed)

P.S. Sorry this shit is so sloppy but hey I was on a role ☺ Send me another picture full body this time ☺ so I can see what you look like head to toe.

(4 Angela)

"4 THOSE NIGHTS WHEN U R ALONE"
by Tupac Shakur

U ever share your soul with a stranger
Only to realize he was a long lost friend?
Ever talk 2 a man like u talk with a woman
And share what you can't with other men?

Can u picture your love being given
2 a criminal stuck in this hell
Can u promise 2 hold off from judging him
Until the day when you really know him well

Can u close your eyes and imagine
If everything went right
The power of passion finally possessed
After all those sleepless nights

I bet u think I'm gaming you
Just like all the men in your past
Cuz' all of them promised u heaven on earth
But none of them seem 2 last

AFTER ALL, WHAT CAN I OFFER U?
Besides Lonely Nights & Sweet words
Promises of pleasures to come
And lines you've already heard

All I can say is have faith in me
And in time maybe you'll come 2 c

The definition and true meaning
Of FRIENDSHIP can be discovered in me

(written exclusively 4 Angela from Tupac Shakur)

P.S. Angie, This is but a small but sincere token of my intentions 4 u Hope u like it It is the only one of it's kind That's on everything I love! No bullshit!

(P.S. Again) What the hell is your last name?

LOVE
Tupac Shakur(signed)

This was a gift—a part of himself—that Tupac was giving me. I feel that poetry is an extension of one's heart and mind. I definitely felt Tupac now.

Tupac,

I am definitely receiving your letters, and I hope you get this one, since you haven't gotten any of the other ones that I've sent. What in the hell are they doing up there with your mail? Eating it? ☺ Don't worry. You are not writing me too much, and you can get as personal as you'd like. I'm fine with that.

I was extremely touched by your letter and the poem, "4 Those Nights When You are Alone." I haven't received poetry from a man since junior high school, and I love poetry. I'll enclose a poem to you. I write a lot of poems and short stories. I'm even working on a book (it's erotic, though). I can write erotic stuff all day, but I don't want it to be so explicit that a normal bookstore won't sell it. Therefore, I'm toning it down.

I don't want you to worry about me thinking that you're bullshitting me because my trust in you will take time to grow. I at least know that you're not saying these things to get in my pants because you can't ☺ (not trying to sound harsh). So I feel you are extending yourself to me, and I accept what you are offering. This will be a special relationship because I've never really had a mental one before. You know, you meet guys, and there is a level, but when it boils down to it, they only want the sex, and that is first and foremost. So, a lot of what they say in conversation you have to ignore because they are gaming. Every female *should* know that, and if they don't . . . well, I do. A lot of men are full of shit. You're right. Hopefully, you won't be part of that group.

I always speak what's on my mind, so if I ever offend you, please let me know. But I can't sit around and bullshit people either. I don't believe in surface relationships on any level, friend or otherwise. If it can't be real, then it might as well not be. Who has time to go through a motion for the hell of it? This is going to be cool. But I have one request, too. If I open up, then you also have to open up. Can you do that? I think you can. ☺

Stay Strong,
Angela

Query

(Written exclusively for Tupac Shakur from Angela)

Can I trust my soul to a stranger?
Someone I hope is going to be a true friend
Can I tell him my sweet secrets?
The ones I can't share with any man

Thoughts of giving my love to someone
Whose mistakes have him stuck in hell
I refuse to judge him from others
I have the opportunity to know him well

I often close my eyes and imagine
When everything is right
The chemistry unleashed between us two
Sparks flying, dim the lights ☺

Skeptical of him on the gaming tip
All men do it so well
No promises needed, no guarantees wanted
Truly time will tell

"After all, what can I offer you?"
Besides pleasant smells and my thoughts
Pictures of wonderment, of if it's all-real
An illusion I am not

All I can say is hang in there
And in the future you will feel
The true, deep meaning of Friendship
In your heart, through your soul, it's real.

I hadn't shared any more information with anyone at the office since the first letter—except, of course, with my roommate. It had become something else to me, and to show the letters around the office every time one came seemed like an invasion of our unification. We were about to share an intimacy that many people don't have an opportunity to share. It was going to be 100 percent mental. In addition, he was Tupac Shakur, and with that came a certain need to be confidential.

Chapter 5

OUR LETTERS CROSS

MARCH 10, 1995

Dearest Angela,

How are you? I still haven't recieved a second letter from you but in my heart I believe it is due to my constant moves in the penile system. I have been moved once again to a MAXIMUM Security Penitentia this time. Clinton Correctional facility. Hopefully if you have written me it will eventually follow me here. I hate 2 complain but this shit is barbaric. I refused to go into the protective custody unit so to punish me the administration has placed me in involuntary P.C. which is worse. They won't let me shower or use the phone. Shit is Rough but as usual! I have faith that God has not brought me this far 2 drop me off in hell. Can u feel me? I miss looking at your picture and smelling your scent. I don't know why but I'm constantly thinking of you, wondering what your doing and who you're doing it with ☺! I know I have no right 2 be so inquisitive about your whereabouts but what can I say, a nigga miss u! That shit feels and sounds so crazy to say and actually know that I miss u and I've never met u, but I do Angela. You'd be surprised how much I got from that 2 minute conversation that seems like so long ago. Your sense of humor, your soft voice and most of all your promise 2 come visit me while I'm locked down. I hope you haven't changed your mind ☺! I hope my instincts about you are right if not then I'm playing myself in major way but shit life aint much without a little risk and danger. So I'm reaching out 2 u, 4 u and I hope you reach back Don't let this time and distance scare you if it's Real it will endure all things. If not, then at worst I'm showing you the inside of a real & true brothA's heart and maybe in the future it will serve you IN some positive method. IN here I'm learning 2 face things that I thought I experienced before but I c Now that I have not. Things like LONLINESS! And from that I'm hoping you can save me. So what do u think. Write me love I Need 2 hear from u. Send it 2 me by FeD ex so a Nigga don't have 2 wait so long. Again I miss u. I mean that. You like how I just made up a last Name 4 u right. It seems to fit. Angela Lovely.

Constantly,
Jupoe G.

P.S. ONE of my "fellow inmates" drew this Envelope up 4 me in exchange of an autograph. what do u think. good deal or what! ☺

Take good care of yourself
settle 4 Nothing less than the best
IN my eyes u deserve it!

ONE Love
2PAC

HOPING U CAN Feel Me!

⟨ An Original & heartfelt poem 4 Angela from Tupac Shakur ⟩

I
I sit alone AND think of u, hoping u can hear me
If I close my eyes Before I sleep I can see u clearly
Even where I am Now, where everything is dark
I can feel you here beside me Tugging at my heart

II
Anxiously I wait 2 hear a precious word or 2.
Something 2 let me Know u feel me as much As I feel u
I take the blame and apologize 4 these Nights that I've denied you
But this gives me time 2 love your mind Before I lay beside you

III
Let me TAKE AWAY your pain, wipe your Tearz and guide u
Let's make Love with pen AND paper Before I come inside u
I hope my words don't sound 2 strong but passion has No fear
Each Breath I Breathe is ecstacy that builds up through the year

IV
There is No cure 4 WHAT 👁 feel It's Just the pain that ails me
No prescribtion from the doctors modern medicine has failed me
And I Know this is alot 2 TAKE But I mean each word Sincerly
These Hungry letters, Sent with passion, Hoping U can feel me

all My Heart ♡
Tupac AL

50

Dearest Angela

How are you? I still haven't received a second letter from you but in my heart I believe it is due to my constant moves in the penile system. I have been moved once again to a Maximum Security Penitentiary this time. Clinton Correctional Facility. Hopefully if you have written me it will eventually follow me here. I hate 2 complain but this shit is barbaric. I refused to go into the protective custody unit so to punish me the administration has placed me in involuntary P.C., which is worse. They won't let me shower or use the phone. Shit is rough but as usual I have faith that God has not brought me this far 2 drop me off in hell. Can you feel me? I miss looking at your picture and smelling your scent. I don't know why but I'm constantly thinking of you, wondering what your doing and who you're doing it with ☺ ! I know I have no right 2 be so inquisitive about your whereabouts but what can I say, a nigga miss u! That shit feels and sounds so crazy to say and actually know that I miss u and I've never met u, but I do Angela. You'd be surprised how much I got from our two-minute conversation that seems like so long ago. Your sense of humor, your soft voice and most of all your promise 2 come visit me while I'm locked down. I hope you haven't changed your mind ☺ ! I hope my instincts about you are right if not then I'm playing myself in a major way but shit life ain't much without a little risk and danger. So I'm reaching out 2 u, 4 u and I hope you reach back. Don't let this time and distance scare you if it's real it will endure all things. If not, then at worst I'm showing you the inside of a real and true brotha's heart and maybe in the future it will serve you in some positive method. In here I'm learning 2 face things that I thought I experienced before but I c now that I have not. Things like LONLINESS! And from that I'm hoping you can save me. So what u think. Write me love I need 2 hear from u. Send it to me Fed ex so a nigga don't have to wait so long. Again I miss u. I mean that. You like how I just made up a last name 4 u right. It seems to fit. <u>Angela Lovely</u>.

Constantly,
Tupac A Shakur (signature)

P.S. ONE of my "fellow inmates" drew this envelope up 4 me in exchange of an autograph. What do you think. Good deal or what! ☺

Take good care of yourself
Settle for nothing less than the best
In my eyes u deserve it!

One Love
2PAC (signed)

HOPING YOU CAN FEEL ME!
<An Original & heartfelt poem 4 Angela from Tupac Shakur>

I sit alone and think of u, hoping you can hear me
If I close my eyes before I sleep I can see you clearly
Even where I am now, where everything is dark
I can feel you here beside me tugging at my heart

Anxiously I wait 2 hear a precious word or 2
Something 2 let me know you feel me as much as I feel u
I take the blame and apologize 4 these nights that I've denied
                    you
But this gives me time 2 love your mind before I lay beside you

Let me take away your pain, wipe your tearz and guide u
Let's make love with pen and paper before I come inside u
I hope my words don't sound 2 strong but passion has no fear
Each breath I breathe is ecstasy that builds up through the year

There is no cure 4 what I feel It's just the pain that ails me
No prescription from the doctors' modern medicine has failed
                    me
And I know this is a lot 2 take but I mean each word sincerely
These hungry letters, sent with passion, Hoping u can feel me

All My Heart,
Tupac A Shakur (signature)

"He still isn't getting my letters," I told my roommate.

"Why?"

"I don't know! If they would stop moving him all over the damn place, then he would get 'em!"

"Where'd they move him now?"

"Somewhere called Clinton Correctional Facility in upstate New York. Do you think they'll forward all the mail I've sent? He doesn't think I'm writing him. He's still talking about our two-minute conversation."

"Well, at least he's still writing," she said.

"But he probably feels like he's writing to himself."

"Well, all you can do is keep writing him until one of your letters gets to him."

I lay across my bed wondering what he was doing. I thought about how alone he probably felt, and how hopeless it seemed that he would ever receive one of my letters. Tanya was right. All I could do was continue to write him and hope that one day they would give him his mail. I turned over, laughing at the thought of him wondering about me. He wants me to save him from the loneliness inside his cell. How?

Tupac,

What in the hell is going on with the mail up there? I've been writing you and sending you poetry, and you're not getting anything? They're going to make me come up there and distribute the mail myself. Are you on a punishment or something ☺? They're probably just messing with you. Don't worry. I have faith that they'll get you my letters—or somebody's letter—soon. I got yours, and I'm kinda surprised that you miss me, but it's nice. It's funny because I find myself racing to the mailbox every day, looking for a letter from you, and I am actually disappointed when I don't get one. I don't know you either, but I think about you a lot, too, and feel that there is a definite connection. And no, I haven't changed my mind about coming to visit. Time will take care of that.

I just want to let you know that I think you are incredibly talented on many levels and that you seem to be a very compassionate individual. I'm deducing this from your letters, not from the media. But I'm sure that the majority of what I'm saying you already know. The question is, do you believe it? We are both a Gemini, so I know what we are capable of on a grand scale. I also know what some of our biggest weaknesses are, and how believing in ourselves is one of the biggest. It seems we never really feel like we're good enough or talented enough. So just in case you don't know, I'm telling you that you are. Nevertheless, I have a feeling that you are quite aware of this ☺, or at least believe your own hype enough to project awareness.

I hope they give you my letters, so we can really start communicating. I'll keep hope alive and will continue to write, and maybe—just maybe—one day you'll get one of these letters.

Get at me!
Angela

P.S. I hope you like my poem!

Dark Corner

(Written exclusively for Tupac Shakur from Angela)

The space around you seems close and closed
Breathing's a luxury you used to know
As you close your eyes and inhale you believe
That the aroma that's suffocating you belongs to me

It dances around you playing blind man's bluff
As you chase the scent catching it's tough
You know you're not crazy, not insane you're aware
But hidden in the darkest corner can you feel me? I'm there

I'm reaching out to you but you can't see
I watch you day in and day out wishing you were free
To see me, to touch me, to talk for hours at a time
But for now the sight of you from my dark corner is fine

Can you feel me Tupac? Know that I'm near
Bring your light to that dark corner no need to fear
What I have for you will make your darkness all-light
Keep your eyes closed feeling my breath on your ear are you alright

You exhale so calmly as I embrace you from behind
You lean your head back so relaxed you've reclined
Breathing steady, mind calm, no disturbance in sight
In our dark corner, I rub your head, you fall asleep, and I bid you
good night.

For a few hours you can release the madness and be free
With your head on my chest my aroma you breathe
Pleasant scents lead to pleasant dreams, so real
I kiss your forehead and rise up as the sunlight breaks the seal

Your eyes open, slow movement, disoriented but relaxed
You look around, not quite sure feeling a bit perplexed
You ask yourself were you dreaming or was someone here last night
As you stare towards the dark corner and realize it's light

Don't worry Tupac darkness will come again
When you'll receive another visit from your newfound friend

So enjoy your days no need to carry on like a mourner
And tonight I'll meet you again in our dark corner

"He's not going to get it," I told my roommate.

"Ann, just mail it and wait."

"I wonder what he's doing right now."

"Probably wondering where the hell all his mail is!" We both looked at each other and started laughing.

"Probably."

"I'm still amazed that he's writing," Tanya said between bites of her lunch.

"Yes, it seemed crazy, but now it feels like I already know him I'm over the initial shock."

"What makes it feel like that—the poetry or something?"

"Yeah, and the flow of the letters, the content. He can't even explain to himself why he's thinking of me. I don't think it's a game."

"You know what's funny?" I smirked.

"What?"

"He's sensitive."

"And?"

"Hello, it's Tupac."

"So . . . and . . . everybody has a sensitive side, Ann."

"I know that, but looking at the television, you don't see it."

"He was sensitive in *Poetic Justice*," she said with a wink, referring to the 1993 movie starring Janet Jackson.

"Tanya, that was acting. I'm serious. I just thought he was so hard and such a knucklehead. But my opinion of him is changing."

"Yeah, I guess so. He still has hardness though." She started smiling.

"Yes, he probably does, but this side is nice, too. It's sexier than the roughneck. No, actually, it's the combination of the two that's sexy."

Chapter 6

MISUNDERSTOOD

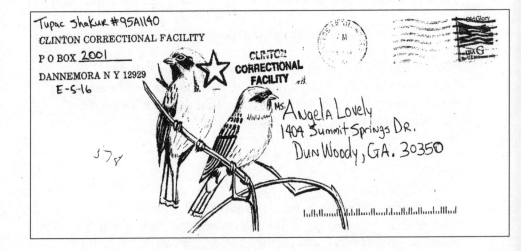

Tupac Shakur #95A1140
CLINTON CORRECTIONAL FACILITY
P O BOX 2001
DANNEMORA N Y 12929
E-5-16

CLINTON
CORRECTIONAL
FACILITY

MS. Angela Lovely
1404 Summit Springs Dr.
Dun Woody, GA. 30350

Dearest Angela,

What's up miss. How ya' feeling? As 4 me it's still "me against the world" and they all out to do me. but as always I'm ready 4 whatever and my only fear of death iz coming back 2 this fucked up world reincarnated. What u been up 2? I still haven't recieved a word back from you yet but if I don't get a reply by the end of this week I'll know there is nothing left 2 be said between us. But I got a hunch I'm just being impatient and I'll get something any day. How'd you like my poems 2 u? they were written with u in mind so let a nigga know what u think. Shit is still dark and cloudy in this midst of this Hell they call Jail but with a little luck you'll supply the Sunshine 2 help a brotha maintain through this dramatic and unfortunate BULLSHIT. I won't keep u long just stay strong. until the next time The World is yours! share with me?

Get At Me,
Tupac C. S.

P.S. WHERE R MY Beautiful Pictures?

If Heaven has a Ghetto

IF ONLY U KNEW MY NATURE
THE ESSENCE OF WHO I AM
MY AMBITIONS R NOW LEGENDARY
BUT I AM A SIMPLE MAN
THE WORLD IS CONVINCED THEY KNOW ME
I'VE BEEN CAPTURED, SHOT AND FRAMED
THEY HAVE CRUCIFIED AND ANALYZED
SACRIFICED AND GAMED ME
BUT I STILL LOVE MY SISTER
GOD FORGIVE HER 4 HER SINS
I WONDER IF HEAVEN HAS A GHETTO
AND WILL THEY LET ME IN?
TOMMORROW IZ NOT PROMISED 2 US
TODAY IZ HARD ENOUGH
HELL AINT SHIT COMPARED 2 LIFE
PROTECT ME GOD IT'z ROUGH!
IF I SHOULD DIE B4 I WAKE
TELL THE YOUTH CAME AND WENT
MY LAST WORDZ HERE WAZ FUCK THE WORLD
BE STRONG AND REPRESENT

MARCH 12, 1995   — TUPAC SHAKUR

WHISPERS   4 Angela

My words will sound like promises
when whispered in your ear
If I gauranteed you ecstacy
Tell me can u wait a year
or give or take a coupla' months
cuz I don't know 4 sure
when the time will come and I'm released
standing outside your door
Awhile back I asked you 2 think of me
at night before you slept
I hope you kept your word 2 me
And the promise 2 me was kept
I can't control what happens now
But patiently I wait
4 U 2 send your heart 2 me.
Inside these prison gates
Let me be your little secret
No one else can know
I'm sending U a piece of me
Hold on and Don't let go
Suspense is what makes things worthwhile
Brings Depth to fantasies
———>

Madness from the lack of contact.
Breeds insanity
Reflecting on a future night
Erractic thoughts appear
But until then I'll ride the wind
Sending Whispers to your ear
                    Tupac O.K.

        Stolen Kisses ☺
Think of me B4 you close your eyes
Allow me inside your Heart
Let me Lay in Bed beside u
and Keep you company in the Dark
Try 2 use your mind 2 imagine me
getting caught up in the midst
Don't be afraid if I get brave
Reach out and Steal a Kiss.
Just 2 see how your Kiss tastE
Temptations of the flesh
And after that we'll both lay back
and Rest Now chest to chest
                    By 2PAC 4 Angela
                    Hope it doesn't offend u
                    write me Back soon!
                                    2PAC

63

Dearest Angela,

What's up miss. How ya' feeling? As 4 me it's still "me Against the world" and they all out to do me but as always I'm Ready 4 whatever and my only fear of death iz coming back 2 this fucked up world reincarnated. What u been up 2? I still haven't received a word back from you yet but if I don't get a reply by the end of this week I'll know there is nothing left to be said between us. But I got a hunch I'm just being impatient and I'll get something any day. How'd you like my poems 2 u? They were written with u in mind so let a nigga know what u think. Shit is still dark and cloudy in this midst of this hell they call jail but with a little luck you'll supply the sunshine 2 help a brotha maintain through this dramatic and unfortunate BULL-SHIT. I won't keep u long just stay strong. Until next time

The world is yours! Share with me!

Get At Me,
Tupac A Shakur (signed)

P.S. Where R My Beautiful Pictures?

IF HEAVEN HAS A GHETTO

IF ONLY YOU KNEW MY NATURE
THE ESSENCE OF WHO I AM
MY AMBITIONS R NOW LEGENDARY
BUT I AM A SIMPLE MAN
THE WORLD IS CONVINCED THEY KNOW ME
I'VE BEEN CAPTURED, SHOT AND FRAMED
THEY HAVE CRUCIFIED AND ANALYZED
SACRIFICED AND GAMED ME
BUT I STILL LOVE MY SISTER
GOD FORGIVE HER FOR HER SINS
I WONDER IF HEAVEN HAS A GHETTO
AND WILL THEY LET ME IN?
TOMMORROW IZ NOT PROMISED 2 US
TODAY IZ HARD ENOUGH
HELL AIN'T SHIT COMPARED TO LIFE
PROTECT ME GOD IT'Z ROUGH!
IF I SHOULD DIE B4 I WAKE
TELL THE YOUTH I CAME AND WENT
MY LAST WORDZ HERE WAZ FUCK THE WORLD
BE STRONG AND REPRESENT

MARCH 12, 1995
Tupac Shakur

4 ANGELA

WHISPERS

My words will sound like promises
When whispered in your ear
If I guaranteed you ecstasy
Tell me can u wait a year
Or give or take a coupla' months
Cuz I don't know for sure
When the time will come and I'm released
Standing outside your door
Awhile back I asked you 2 think of me
At night before you slept
I hope you kept your word 2 me
And the promise 2 me was kept
I can't control what happens now
But patiently I wait
4 u 2 send your heart to me
Inside these prison gates
Let me be your little secret
No one else can know
I'm sending u a piece of me
Hold on and don't let go
Suspense is what makes things worthwhile
Brings depth to fantasies
Madness from the lack of contact
Breeds insanity
Reflecting on the future night
Erratic thoughts appear
But until then I'll ride the wind
Sending whispers to your ear

Tupac A Shakur (signed)

STOLEN KISSES ☺

Think of me b4 you close your eyes
Allow me inside your heart
Let me lay in bed beside u
And keep you company in the dark
Try 2 use your mind 2 imagine me
Getting caught up in the midst
Don't be afraid if I get brave
Reach out and steal a kiss
Just 2 see how your kiss taste
Temptations of the flesh
And after that we'll both lay back
And rest now chest to chest

By 2PAC 4 Angela

Hope it doesn't offend u
Write me back soon!
Tupac

Tupac,

I am so frustrated that you have received only one of my letters. This doesn't make any sense. Well, I hope that some-body's letters are shortening your days. I want you to know that I truly appreciate your realness. It's refreshing. Many guys walk around thinking their transparent game is tight. They have only one goal that matters to them: locate, aim, and fire their little raggedy weapons, and damn the target after they've bombed it. I know I sound bitter, but I'm keep-ing it real, too. I feel we are about to embark on some other level. But to follow your words, "I hope my instincts about you are right if not then I'm playing myself . . . but life ain't much without a little risk and danger." I'll get back to getting acquainted with you.☺ Here are some breakdown ques-tions for you: Do you think you have a typical Gemini per-sonality? How is your temper? Are you moody? Do you snore? What is a sexy woman to you? What are the most important features of a woman? What are your views on re-lationships? In your relationships, do you tend to be more traditional or more unorthodox? How are you on the love thing? Are you a true Gemini in the sex department? ☺ Is sex physical or mental for you? What's your favorite part of foreplay? How experimental are you? Where do you see yourself in the next five years?

It's funny. I am a romantic at heart, and your poetry is touching every angle of it. It's nice to see a man who is com-fortable enough with himself to express his feelings in po-etry or in general. I hope that it continues and that your inhibitions, if you have any, remain locked away, never to enter our pages or conversations. Hope will either kill you or make you stronger. Let's go for stronger, shall we? ☺ Tell me what you're thinking.

Forever,
Angela

I Wait

(Written exclusively for Tupac from Angela)

You say shit is still dark and cloudy in the midst of this hell they call
jail
But with a little luck I'll supply the sunshine you need to get you
through when all else fails
I'll help a brotha maintain through his dramatic and unfortunate
bullshit
With elements of mental pleasures and visual stimuli as I see fit

You told me the world was mine and to share some with you
So I'm positioning my pen on a has-been piece of clean paper to
distribute some to you
Are you feeling me through the lines that form letters and words
put together as thoughts
Are you finding the spirit within the expressions [effects that] shouldn't
be fought

You asked for this from me on more than one occasion
I'm opening myself up to you no more need for persuasion
Buckle down, focus hard, release your mind, and embrace this gift
No worries, no lies, no disillusions, sit tight as we shift

To another level where our minds expose our souls
On the pages of each letter we begin to fill invisible holes
That led to our voids and needs giving a chance to escape with
words
Freeing ourselves as we soar to the highest heights gliding like birds

Are you ready Tupac for all that you have asked
Speak up now and just know it's not too late to pass

Time's running out as I wait for your response and your key
To the expressions of your soul that have the power to set us both
free
I wait . . .

"That's beautiful, honey," my mom said hesitantly.

"What's wrong?" I asked.

"Well, Angela, you don't know anything about him and you're talking about going to see him."

"Mom, that's what the letter writing is about. It's not like I'm going tomorrow."

"What I've heard about him doesn't make him seem cool at all."

"The media is the media. I'm making, and will make, my own judgments based on our letters. It could be fake on his part, but I'll feel it out. You know me. Didn't we already have this conversation?" I said, laughing.

"Yes, we did, and I do know you."

"He's harmless, Mom. Don't worry," I said, trying to reassure her. I was beginning to believe that.

"So now you're going to be the one to save him from himself?"

"No. Only he can save himself from himself. We're going to be friends. He's going through difficult times, and I want to help, if I can. What's the big deal?" There was a long pause on the other end of the phone.

"Well, I know you're going to do what you want, so be careful."

"Mom, he's harmless."

"Okay. So how was work?" We talked for over an hour, not bringing up Tupac again. As a mother, she had every right to worry, based on the depictions of him in the media.

There was something very relaxing about this situation, but I couldn't put my finger on it. He was hungry for something I had, and the fact that he was still writing confirmed it. He was filled with hope and impatience at receiving my mail. This was loud and clear in all of his letters. I was finished trying to figure out why he was still writing. This was an inevitable situation, and our lives were touching by design.

Chapter 7

A REQUEST

"Hello," I said into the phone. I had been lounging in the tub, enjoying a bath and talking to my friend, when a second call interrupted.

"Hello, Ms. Lovely," Tupac said with a smile in his voice.

A smile spread across my face from ear to ear, and my heart began to beat triple time.

"Tupac! Oh my God! They took you off punishment?" I joked. We both laughed.

"Yeah, they did, I guess. Watchu doin', Ms.?" he asked. At that moment, I realized that I had forgotten my friend on the other line.

"Oh! Hey, hold on for one second, okay?"

"Yeah," he said, and I clicked to the other line.

"Hey, I'll call you back in a minute," I told my friend.

"You still haven't told me where you want to go eat," he said.

"I have to call you back, or better yet, just come over in about thirty minutes and we'll figure it out when you get here," I said, frustrated. "Okay? Bye." I clicked back over to Tupac.

"Hey," I crooned.

"What's up?"

"Nothing. Did you get my letters yet?"

"Nope. I thought you gave up on me. I was kinda callin' to see if you had or if I was bein' impatient," he said.

"Impatient, Pac. I wouldn't do that. I have no reason to give up. I've sent you like five or six letters with pictures and poetry. I sent you a card and . . ."

"You wrote me poetry?" he interrupted.

"Yeah!" I said. He started laughing. "What's so funny?" I asked.

"You sound sexy when you're frustrated," he joked.

"Well, you should hear me when I'm mad. You'd swear you had just had phone sex!" We both laughed.

"It's good to hear your voice. They just gave me my phone privileges back," he said.

I found my way out of the tub and onto my bed. "If they took all of your stuff when they moved you and haven't given it back to you yet, and you haven't received any of my letters, how were you able to write me, let alone call me now?" I questioned, putting on lotion.

"I wrote your address and phone number on my arm," he said, smiling. "I tried rubbing your letter on my clothes for the smell, but it didn't work." We both laughed.

"You're silly," I said, still laughing. "Oh, yeah, and I want to let you know that I love your poetry."

"I'm glad you like it. There's a lot more where that came from," he assured.

"Good. It's funny 'cause I've started looking forward to getting my mail now," I said, putting on my jeans and shirt.

"Yeah, me too, but I've been fucked up because none of the ones I'm getting are from you."

"Well, I hope they release my letters to you soon."

"Me, too. I think about you so much. I can't explain it. Does it scare you? The intenseness of my letters?" he asked, as I stared at my naked face in the mirror.

"No, I like it. It seems crazy that two weeks ago we didn't know each other and now we're on the phone with this electricity thing happening."

"Yeah. So you do feel it, too?" he asked.

"Oh, yeah, I feel it, and you're right that it's hard to explain. Maybe I knew you in a past life."

"Right," he said, laughing.

"My mom is leery of this whole thing. She's afraid for me with you," I said.

"Why?" He sounded hurt. "I wouldn't do anything to hurt you," he said.

"I know, Boo. It's just a mama thing. She wouldn't be one if she wasn't concerned. Don't worry about it, though. It has no bearing on our thang," I assured him.

"I'm glad. I wish I was there just to look at you," he said quietly.

"That would be nice," I responded, lying across my bed.

"Do you think we'll make it until I get out? You know how Geminis are. We build up things, then lose interest after the curiosity dies," he said.

"I know. Let's just hope that more than curiosity grows here."

"I guess we'll just take it one letter at a time. Well, at least this situation will give me a chance to take my time with you," he said.

"I can handle that. Do me a favor," I said.

"What's that?" he said.

"Will you write me a more personal letter? It doesn't have to reveal any dark secrets, but I'd just like to know you more than on the surface," I said.

"I can do that, Ms. Lovely. Well, I have to go now. Write me and send me more pictures."

"I'm trying, but they won't give 'em to you!"

"Please keep trying. At least now I know you didn't give up on me," he said softly.

"Just know that I never will," I whispered.

"I don't know how I'm supposed to sleep tonight with you sounding like that," he joked. We both laughed.

"Peacefully, I hope, with nothing but pleasant thoughts," I said seductively.

"See, now you playin'. That's cool, Ms. Lovely, that's cool," he said with a chuckle. I could hear some voices in the background, but I couldn't make out what they were saying.

"They're buggin' out. I have to go before they take away my phone privileges again."

"All right."

"Don't forget our star tonight," he said.

"I'll meet you there at midnight."

"Bye."

"Bye."

I hung up the phone and stretched out on my bed. I felt like someone had just given me fabulous foreplay.

TUPAC SHAKUR # 95A1140
CLINTON CORRECTIONAL FACILITY
P O BOX 2001 '
DANNEMORA N Y 12929
E-5-16

MS ANGELA LOVELY
1404 Summit Springs Drive
Dunwoody, GA. 30350

MISS U!
TPAC

March 17, 1995

My Dearest Angela, 👁️ Have just finished our brief and torturous conversation and I'm going crazy with thoughts, hopes and fantasies concerning you. In all honesty I can't explain this effect U have on my brain but it's intoxicating and hard 2 shake. I spend so many of my countless hours here in anticipation of seeing you 4 the first time, touching U 4 the first time laughing, eating and waking up with U 4 the first time the crazy shit is the way my ♥ feels U would think I've already made love 2 U and I've known U 4 years but it's that deep. Do 👁️ scare U like I scare your mother? Please inform your mother that I was greatly disturbed by the fact that she "feared" me. If only she knew how truly unthreatening my nature is. But I understand her apprehension, with the violent picture the media has painted my image in my music & movies and the countless immature acts I have committed it's enough 2 cause certain feelings of caution. However, if it's cool with her I would like 2 extend an invitation 4 dinner 2 her so that she can see 4 herself what is in my heart. The only drawback is my confinement limits my engagements for at least a year and 1/2 but if she's still worried after my release 4 her daughter's safety then I respectfully request she take me up on my offer of a home cooked meal. Even she knows criminals don't cook so that clears me up right there ☺ Now back to my primary source of attention Ms Angela! Do you know how fucked up 👁️ was over the beauty of your voice, the pleasure of hearing your laugh only made it that much rougher 2 get through the night, But you know how the saying goes. Absence makes the heart grow fonder ☺ Besides like I said over the phone

①

👁 Want 2 do Something with U that I've Never done with Any other female - TAKE MY TIME! Being that I'm physically Incarcerated only helps my Motives because As sexy as your Voice is and as pretty as your perfume smells I would have broken my willpower's promise In weeks so This cell Is good 4 Something After All huh? Now have u been thinking of me As u promised me? EVERY Night? Even when there's someone else laying Beside U? Be Honest Now! I feel like A Kid iN high School every time the mail comes By I'm hoping + Anticipating it's from you. I'm Sniffing the bundles of mail I recieve Searching 4 that familiar return Adress but each day brings disappointment yet even though we are New friends I have faith iN U and can't Nothing or Nobody tell me there isn't a Small fire burning between us. And on everything I love I promise U if u make it through this difficult year and a ½ then I will do my best 2 make all these dayz and nights up 2 U and No Matter what else life brings We will, if I have Anything 2 do with it, Remain TRUE FRIENDZ CaN U feel me? You asked me 2 write U a personal letter well let me see — Well Personally I don't know where 2 begin ☺ Just Kidding!

TupAc Amaru Shakur born June 16, 1971 to Afeni Shakur and Kenneth Saunders (deceased) was from birth destined 2 C a prison cell. My mother was pregnant with me on trail for several bullshit charges stemming from her involvement with the BLACK PANTHERS. Eventually she would serve as her own attorney facing 360 years and win an aquital. My Father A street hustler and gangster was impressed by this short haired dark skinned militant woman and they had a brief pretty boy "fling" Just enough 4 My moms 2 fall in love with this Ruff Neck and 4 him 2 impregnate her. So 9 months toss my Dogs disappears And after sevrai miscarriages

②

I was thrust into this world. All of my mother's pain, loneliness and desperation, was fed 2 me and thus I was a quiet and sensitive child, with no male role models. I was my mother's joy until I reached puberty during which time my sister was born from the sperm of a fellow militant. He too would leave my mother. Anyway by puberty I begun to take on the characteristics of my "gangster" father and I took to the streets, nothing serious just constantly in search of a male role model 2 guide me into manhood. Like many single parent black families we were forced into a life of poverty after all of the militant blacks quit the movement in search of "real" lives. Bitter and abandoned my mother held out 4 as long as she could and then finally succumbed 2 drugs. Around this time I was entering my second year of the prestigious Baltimore School 4 the Performing Arts. We had long since left New York homeless and peniless. In my 12th grade year of high school with my college applications in hand I came home 2 find all the electricity and lights had been turned off and my mother with a black eye. The reason my father and all of the other men left my moms was because she was strong and dominating so needless 2 say the sight of my hero with a black eye was a traumatic experience 4 me. The next day with 4 chicken wings and 5 dollars (her last) I was put on a greyhound bus 4 california 2 stay with a family friend. Seeing my mother and the condition I left her in left an impression I can never erase from my mind. Anyway I went 2 california naive and basically a mama's boy. I was introduced 2 the real street life by getting jumped because I tried 2 intervene as a drug dealer beat up his girl. I got my ass kicked and she was back with him before my eye could heal. (I learned a valuable lesson here!) After a ③

Painful year of lessons like this I became a
petty criminal (weed sales, fights, etc.) However because
of my good nature I was not sucessful. I never
collected my debts, I let people slide I basically was
a failure. I ran into an older white lady (married) who
took a liking 2 me and looked out 4 me financially
as long as I gave her some dick occassionaly. Anyway
2 make a long story short she introduced me 2
some people they liked my rapping & took me on tour
as a roadie (Basically a flunkie) this group was digital underground
through hardwork and determination 👀 went from carrying
thier luggage 2 Rapping on their next albulm. I recieved
alot of rave reviews and a small following and released
my first albulm 2PACALYPSE NOW then by stroke of
luck I stumbled into an audition 4 a new movie called Juice
I got the lead role and thus the legend of 2Pac was
born. Showing my appreciation 9 the criminals who supported
me I founded thug life and tried 2 handle this
newfound fame. Which leads me 2 where I am now
still trying 2 handle the flames of fame. There's
so much more but soon the mystery will be gone
and I need 2 keep your attention 4 at least a year
when I can occupy it some other wayz! 😊

P.S.
Is this
personal,!?
enough.

Passionately
2Pac

④

This one is 4 U & Your Mother, Really Your Mother!

TELL MAMA

A MAN IS MADE OF MANY THINGS
None of which CAN Be Seen AT A GLANCE
EVEN A ROSE CAN grow FROM concrete
if WATERED AND given the CHANCE

WHEN Judging A MAN FiRST TAKe iN Account
The CONDiTiONS FROM WHiCH He's prevailed
His Ability 2 Keep the faith
Not Just iN Victory, but when He fails

Tell Mama please Don't worry
There's No Need 4 Caution Here
4 I was Born an honorable man
So there's Nothing 4 her 2 FeaR

Never Judge A Book by it's cover
I'm Sure she's heard that B4
AND WHAT Would life Be like 4 US
If we were all 2 Scared 2 explore

So Dare 2 DO WHAT NO oNe HAS DONe
GeT 2 KNOW M E B4 U JUDge ME
9 times out of 10, we'll become friends
AND in time Maybe U 2 will love me ☺

Respectfully
Tupoc C.S
⑤

IF ONLY WE R PATIENT ! 4 Angela !

Tonight though I sleep in Solitude
My thoughts are filled with you
I wonder After this iNSANiTY
Do fantasies come True

Will my words communicate my wishes
These passionate slow kisses
ANticipated love embraces
As Magical as this is

Explosive Nights of love making
each time a different lesson
The MOON will guide my every STROKE
I'm Blessed By your expressions

Draped in Sweat chest 2 chest
A climax 2 our frustration
This is the Reward that We caN Both Share
If only we are patient . . . . . .

P.S. THIS Ain't
The ONE 2
SHOW MAMA ! ☺

Constantly
CPC

P.S.S. I Hope U R SAViNG All of my letters & Poems
AND keeping These 2 yourself ☺ !

⑥

March 17, 1995

My Dearest Angela,

    I have just finished our brief and torturous conversation and I'm going crazy with thoughts, hopes and fantasies concerning you. In all honesty I can't explain this effect u have on my brain but it's intoxicating and hard 2 shake. I spend so many countless hours here in anticipation of seeing you 4 the first time, Touching u 4 the first time, laughing, eating and waking up with u 4 the first time the crazy shit is the way my heart feels u would think I've already made love 2 u and I've known u 4 years but it's that deep. Do I scare u like I scare your mother? Please inform your mother that I was greatly disturbed by the fact that she "feared" me. If only she knew how truly unthreatening my nature is. But I understand her apprehension, with the violent picture the media has painted my image in music & movies and the countless immature acts I <u>have</u> committed it's enough 2 cause certain feelings of caution. However, if it's cool with her I would like 2 extend an invitation 4 dinner 2 her so that she can see 4 herself what is in my heart. The only drawback is my confinement limits my engagements for at least a year and ½, but if she's still worried after my release 4 her daughter's safety then I respectfully request she take me up on my offer of a home cooked meal. Even she knows criminals don't cook so that clears me up right there ☺. Now back to my primary source of attention Ms. Angela! Do you know how fucked up I was over the beauty of your voice, the pleasure of hearing your laugh only made it that much rougher 2 get through the night. But you know how the saying goes Absence makes the heart grow fonder ☺.

Besides like I said over the phone I want 2 do something with u that I've never done with any other female—TAKE MY TIME! Being that I'm physically incarcerated only helps my motives because as sexy as your voice is and as pretty as your perfume smells, I would have broken my willpower's promise in weeks so this cell is good 4 something after all Huh? Now have u been thinking of me as u promised me? Every night? Even when there's someone else laying beside u? Be honest now! I feel like a kid in high school every time the mail comes by. I'm hoping and anticipating it's from you. I'm sniffing the bundles of mail I receive searching 4 that familiar return address but each day brings disappointment yet even though we are new friends I have faith in u and can't nothing or nobody tell me there isn't a small fire burning between us. And on everything I love I promise u if u make it through this difficult year and ½ then I will do my best 2 make all these dayz and nights up 2 u and no matter what else life brings we will, if I have anything to do with it, remain TRUE FRIENDZ. Can u feel me? You asked me 2 write u a personal letter well let me see ———

Well <u>personally</u> I don't know where 2 begin ☺ Just Kidding!

Tupac Amaru Shakur born June 16, 1971 to Afeni Shakur and Kenneth Saunders (deceased) was from birth destined 2 C a prison cell. My mother was pregnant with me on trial for several bullshit charges stemming from her involvement with the BLACK PANTHERS. Eventually she would serve as her own attorney facing 360 years and win an acquittal. My father a street hustler and gangster was impressed by this short haired dark skinned militant woman and they had a brief "fling" Just enough 4 my moms

2 fall in love with this pretty boy ruffneck and 4 him 2 impregnate her. So 9 months pass my pops disappears and after several miscarriages I was thrust into this world. All of my mother's pain, loneliness and desperation was fed 2 me and thus I was a quiet and sensitive child, with no male role models, I was my mother's joy until I reached puberty during which time my sister was born from the sperm of a fellow militant. He too would leave my mother. Anyway by puberty I began to take on the characteristics of my "gangster" father and I took to the streets, nothing serious just constantly in search of a male role model 2 guide me into manhood. Like many single parent black families we were forced into a life of poverty after all of the militant blacks quit the movement in search of "real" lives. Bitter and abandoned my mother held out 4 as long as she could and then finally succumbed 2 drugs. Around this time I was entering my second year of the prestigious Baltimore School 4 the Performing Arts. We had long since left New York homeless and penniless. In my 12th grade year of high school with my college applications in hand, I came home 2 find all the electricity and lights had been turned off and my mother with a black eye. The reason my father and all of the other men left my moms was because she was strong and dominating so needless to say the sight of my Hero with a black eye was a traumatic experience 4 me. The next day with 4 chicken wings and $5 dollars (her last) I was put on a greyhound bus 4 California 2 stay with a family friend seeing my mother and the condition I left her in left an impression I can never erase from my mind. Anyway I went 2 California naïve and basically a mama's boy. I was introduced 2 the real Street Life by getting jumped because I tried 2 intervene as a drug dealer beat up his girl. I got my ass kicked and

she was back with him before my eye could heal. (I learned a valuable lesson here!) After a painful year of lessons like this I became a petty criminal (weed sales, fights, etc!) However because of my good nature I was not successful. I never collected my debts, I let people slide I basically was a failure. I ran into an older white lady (married) who took a liking to me and looked out 4 me financially as long as I gave her some dick occasionally. Anyway to make a long story short, she introduced me 2 some people, they liked my rapping and took me on tour as a roadie (basically a flunky). This group was digital underground. Through hard work and determination I went from carrying their luggage 2 rapping on their next album. I received a lot of rave reviews and a small following and released my first album 2PACALYPSE NOW then by stroke of luck I stumbled into an audition 4 a new movie called Juice. I got the lead role and thus the legend of 2PAC was born. Showing my appreciation 4 the criminals who supported me I founded THUGLIFE and tried 2 handle this new-found fame. Which leads me 2 where I am now still trying 2 handle the flames of fame. There's so much more but soon the mystery will be gone and I need 2 keep your attention 4 at least a year when I can occupy it some other wayz! ☺

Passionately
2PAC (signed)

P.S. Is this personal enough!?

4 Angela

IF ONLY WE R PATIENT!

Tonight, though I sleep in solitude
My thoughts are filled with you
I wonder after this insanity
Do fantasies come true

Will my words communicate my wishes
These passionate slow kisses
Anticipated love embraces
As magical as this is

Explosive nights of love making
Each time a different lesson
The moon will guide my every stroke
I'm blessed by your expressions

Draped in sweat chest 2 chest
A climax 2 our frustration
This is the reward that we can both share
If only we are patient . . . . . .

P.S. THIS AIN'T THE ONE 2 SHOW MAMA! ☺

Constantly
2PAC (signed)

P.S.S. I HOPE YOU ARE SAVING ALL OF MY LETTERS &
POEMS AND KEEPING THESE 2 YOURSELF ☺!

This one is 4 u & your mother, Really Your Mother
TELL MAMA

A MAN IS MADE OF MANY THINGS
None of which can be seen at a glance
Even a rose can grow from concrete
If watered and given the chance

When judging a man first take in account
The conditions from which he's prevailed
His ability 2 keep the faith
Not just in victory, but when he fails

Tell Mama please don't worry
There's no need 4 caution here
4 I was born an honorable man
So there's nothing 4 her 2 fear

Never judge a book by its cover
I'm sure she's heard that B4
And what would life be like 4 us
If we were all 2 scared 2 explore

So dare 2 do what no one has done
Get 2 know me B4 U judge me
9 times out of 10, we'll become friends
And in time maybe u 2 will love me ☺

Respectfully,
Tupac A Shakur (signed)

Pac,

I'm glad that you wrote my information on your arm. Otherwise, I probably would have thought you weren't interested, too. In your letter, you asked me if you scare me. In the beginning, I was nervous writing you, even though I didn't really think that you would respond. Then when you did, well, I had my fears of who you might be. However, in my heart I believed you were good, and I was right. You have enlightened me, and you make me smile. I hope I can make you smile in the place that needs a boost, too.

I don't want you to worry about my mother not liking you. Right now, it has no bearing on anything. It will take her some time to grasp what is happening, and until she does, she can't really begin to break away from how the media has conditioned her to view you through its fabulous portrayal of you ☺. However, she thanks you for the dinner invite and says she'll think about it when the time comes. You cook, too? You're a man of many talents. Speaking of cooking, I almost burned the house down. I came home from the gym late and was starving, so I put on some beanie weenies and went and laid down. When I woke up, the alarm was going off, my beanie weenies had burned, and I was still hungry. ☺ Luckily, my roommate was home.

Oh! I have kept my promise to you, even when someone's been present. There is a definite heat here, Pac. It was good talking to you, and I wish we could have talked all night. Your letter was definitely personal enough. I wasn't expecting that much information. Thank you for sharing yourself with me. Hey! Psst . . . psst . . . Tupac. Meet me in our dark corner tonight, okay?

Forever,
Angela

P.S. I love the poetry, Pac. I'm feeling special!!!!!!!!

Chapter 8

GETTING PERSONAL (AND SHOCKED)

TuPAC Shakir # 95A1140
CLINTON CORRECTIONAL FACILITY
P O BOX 2001
DANNEMORA N Y 12929
E-5-16

Ms. Angela Ardis
1404 Summit Springs Dr.
Dunwoody GA. 30350

CLINTON
CORRECTIONAL
FACILITY

Old Glory
G

TELL your mother
there's no need 2
worry or fear.
2PAC

you'll Always be Ms. Lovely
2 me!
☺

MARCH 18, 1995

Dearest Angela,

Let's C, where do 👁 Begin? First of off I finally recieved your letters and As God As my witness I was thoroughly overjoyed. Damn, I laughed, blushed, smiled, thought, and smirked 4 at least 3 hours. It's alot 2 answer but I'm going 2 take my time and try 2 deal with every point you raised. In Case my last letter wasn't personal enough here's my "breakdown" (as u put it)

① Personality: I am extremely good natured, Adventurous and much more than just free spirit Sometimes I'm down right dangerous with my open mind and heart (As u already know) I have an uncanny ability 2 use my heart 2 guide me toward expected happiness. Sometimes I'm Sucessful and Sometimes I learn painful lessons. I can be very serious but life is so damn cruel that I plunge myself into bouts with silliness and horseplay (it allows me 2 experience my childhood which I have never really had.) I'm beyond dependable 2 those worthy of my trust I have been known 2 challenge the world and move mountains 2 defend or assist my friends. I'M generous to the point it drains me financially Sometimes. I financially take care of my Mother, Aunt, Uncle, female Cousin Jamala, Sista Sekyiwa, Cousins; Kateri, Malcolm, Dena, Nelson, Helema, Billy, Kenny, and Many others 2 many 2 name I also have unformally adopted an orphaned young black male name Mootaw who now lives at my house in Atlanta. I have given my friends Benz' (300 CE) brand new and all kinds of Jewelry

I've given my sister the deed 2 my house (cuz she was pregnant) and covered all prenatal care 4 her and my cousin as well as all other bills and things. I've bought my mom's and Aunt cars as well as my Uncle and cousins. That's just my nature 2 give all that I can 2 those that I love. I've given bums 100 dollar bills and strangers have been treated 2 dinner at 4 star resturants on numerous occassions. I'm not a trick I'm just good hearted and believe in sharing that's the good side Now on my flip side I'm no Joke I can cold hearted, merciless, and relentless in my pursuit of revenge when pushed 2 the point. But I only strike out in self defense I have NEVER harmed anyone or anything unless they were meaning 2 do me harm first. I'm Honest almost to a fault. I say exactly what I feel sometimes without thinking of the outcome (as you have seen). So in a Nutshell that's my Personality. Mix in a little Mishief, Passion, intelligence, and Sensitivity and you can almost feel me! Neat!

2 Health: After getting shot I started 2 workout a little but before that I didn't do shit. No wieghts, No push ups, Nothing. I eat like an animal but can't seem 2 gain more than 165 pounds (go figure!) I eat pork (Don't tell nobody :) And I love RIBS. Besides All of that I'm healthy thank God

(cont)
Before getting shot I've never been sick or even had a cold. I've been lucky. Sexually I've never been given a sexually transmitted disease and I have never passed one on either ☺. I have been tested 4 aids (since the shooting) and I am negative. I have perfect vision I run fast, I love hard, and I don't snore. ☺ Next!

~~Men~~ I mean ③ Women ☺: I LOVE BEAUTIFUL WOMEN. From the curve in thier backs to the length of thier nails. I love the little things as much as the big ones. I love lingerie, slow kisses, passionate lovemaking and romantic dinners. I CAN COOK better than most women (including my mother and aunt) and I enjoy cooking 4 that special someone but that's a treat. I like the breasts of a woman the most then her hair and nails. The mouth is very important to me almost as major as the eyes. I love eyes and deep eye contact. My favorite trait of a woman is her voice. The sweetness and softness of her tone and of course a sense of humor that's very important. Like u said the chemistry is infinite but once I feel it it's on 4 real! Next

⟶

93

④ Relationships: Here's where I may lose U.
Whether we're friends, fuck buddies (as you so frankly put it)
or man and woman (I'm too old 2 be anybody's boyfriend :) it
has to be intense. 2 be honest I have never had just
a friend or just a lover or just a woman. I want
all three in one. I'm very greedy but not over imposing.
I believe in the old fashioned system. There can only
be one dominant presence in a relationship at least
as far as masculinity goes and that's for a man.
My woman should make me her priority and love me
with every drop of spit in her mouth no exceptions.
Without passion I become bored so there must
be a constant elevation of intensity between us.
There can be no secrets between her and I.
The only time I should be unsure of her next
move is in bed. I give a lot to my relationships
I have sometimes been known to give too much
but it is only because I love deeply not in
pieces & bits. I have been in love but never
have I stayed in love. Women tend to
relax when they feel they "have" me and shit
breaks down. I'm big on communication from
our hopes and dreams to the position you prefer
in bed. (I'll get into that in the Sex section)
2 me every relationship is both a lesson
and a journey unique in every way. Next

⑤ Love : This one is difficult.

I can fall in love in a matter of days and on the other hand it can take years b4 I truly love someone. It depends on the intensity factor. A woman has to conquer my heart, mind and body (in that order) b4 I can truly say I love her but once done it's hard 2 fall out of love unless she was pretending or being false in some way. I can love a woman 4 many reasons. Maybe 4 what I can give 2 her or make her into or even vice versa 4 what she can make me into or share with me. I have loved young ghetto girls and older Rich girls all in different ways. As far as my ideal woman, I'm not too sure. First of all she must be faithful in every way. Not just with her body but faithful in the sense that regardless of where she is or who she's with she must represent me in the utmost. She has to be woman enough to allow me 2 control our situation in public. it is disrespectful 2 me 2 c a woman arguing with a man while she with her man. feel me? Not my slave but my partner. there can only be one driver in the car. When a woman allows her man to represent her in public it shows other men ♦ her satisfaction and respect 4 her man. Let's say 4 example we're at dinner and the waiter brings you the wrong meal. instead of you dealing with it, your man handles the situation 4 u. feel me? On the other hand suppose we're out and a guy comes on

(cont)

2 U. Instead of the man intervening, it is on the woman
2 put the man in place in a sweet way sparring his
feelings. This shows security in the relationship.
Basically I dislike loud women or jealous women it's
a major turn off. My women has 2 understandin
my profession women come at me constantly. If she's
secure there's no need 2 be rude or selfish
she should be happy I am loved by so many
this is my business and it affects not just me
but us as a couple. This part is deep but
hopefully u get the drift if not I'll explain it
in depth in a separate letter. Next.

(6) SEX! (this is where the fun starts)

4 me sex is deep and mental. It's much more
than in and out, up and down bumb & grind.
Foreplay is the foundation for pleasurable love
making. The kiss tells it all. I love 2 kiss
not just on the mouth but the entire body.
the elbows, the back of the knees, the neck, the ears
the breasts and every inch in between. Variety
is the major part. I like 2 make love on the bed
in the kitchen, in the shower, on the floor wherever
the passion moves us. I like 2 do it slow but
I change speeds with the intensity. Positions

96

Help to bring pleasure in ways No one can imagine, but even before intercourse I like to tease the woman with my dick (excusemyfrench) barely slipping it in and then pulling it out. I like to use my tongue 2 explore her whole body prolonging the act to the point of torture. Anticipation brings ecstacy! I like to hold the woman throughout the entire act, sometimes firmly and at other times softly. I like 2 use Ice, honey, whip cream, cucumbers, anything 2 add variety. Blindfolds and soft ropes are exciting. As well as coughdrops and icecream. I like 2 be dominant and submissive. Loud and quiet. When making love the gemini comes out of me I can be gently making love in one moment and passionately fucking your brains out in the next. I love getting kissed on my neck licked on my chest and sucked well ... you know what I mean. Basically as you can see I'm deep into making love. I like quickies as well as long passionate sessions of lovemaking like I said variety is the key. Well Now that I'm all sweaty and horny let's move on!

:)

Turn the page this page is hot as hell :)

You alright? Hope I didn't scare you away. You must be like "Damn this nigga is a stone cold freak!" well your half right (I'm not cold at all 😊) Anyway back 2 u. that's enough of me and what I like, I read what you asked of me in your last letter (your favor) well it's done! Each and every night you'll get that moment. I keep trying 2 tell myself not 2 speak of sex in my letters and in the future I'll do less of that, that's a promise! Now Do me a favor. The next time your out with your "friends". Out of nowhere tell'em 2PAC said Hi and let me know thier response. It has 2 be when they don't expect it. Can u do that 4 me? Please?

I got all your pictures in my locker bringing Sunshine 2 my dreary cell but like I said "I'm greedy" so send more when u can. Remember Variety is the key! I think I covered the profile part. By the way u will never know the sensations I got when you called me "Boo" in your last letter (whew) 😊! Be careful in the kitchen, love don't burn the spot down before I get to see it. Oh u asked me what my 5 year plan was so Here it is!

IN 5 years I WANT TO RULE The World!

Is that too much? Seriously, I want to write, Act, and direct my own movies, I want to write, produce and perform my own Albulms (completed) I want to manage and produce other groups (completed) and I also want to establish →

A youth program called "US FIRST" and build and run a Center called "GHETTO HEAVEN" and put out a magazine called "GHETTO GOSPEL" at the same time open a resturant, Buy another House, Another BMW, and Find the WOMAN 2 be my Queen in this Kingdom I will Build. Is that 2 much? I'm already half way Finished with most of this and the rest is in the works upon my release. SHIT DON'T STOP! the World is ours! In my Next letter I'll explain my Youth program 2 U. I remember you said ~~that~~ "It's all about the Youth" & Keep YA HEAD UP. Keep me in your heart & mind and Never sleep until you've thought of us together, Promise Me! Sleep good tonight! I miss you Ms. Angela "Lovely" Ardis

ETERNALLY,

Tupac Amaru Sh

My Real Name! Who could make this up! ☺ ——> Tupac Amaru Shakur
6-16-71
Constantly thinking of U!

March 18. 1995

Dearest Angela,

Let's C, where do I begin? First of off I finally received your letters and as God as my witness I was thoroughly overjoyed. Damn, I laughed, blushed, smiled, thought, and smirked 4 at least 3 hours. It's a lot 2 answer but I'm going to take my time and try 2 deal with every point you raised. In case my last letter wasn't personal enough here's my "breakdown" (as u put it).

PERSONALITY: I am extremely good natured, adventurous and much more than just free spirit sometimes I'm down right dangerous with my open mind and heart (as u already know) I have an uncanny ability 2 use my heart 2 guide me toward expected happiness. Sometimes I'm successful and sometimes I learn painful lessons. I can be very serious but life is so damn cruel that I plunge myself into bouts of silliness and horseplay (it allows me 2 experience my childhood which I have never really had). I'm beyond dependable 2 those worthy of my trust I have been known to challenge the world and move mountains 2 defend or assist my friends. I'm generous to the point it drains me financially sometimes. I financially take care of my mother, aunt, uncle, female cousin Jamala, sista Sekyiwa, Cousins; Malcolm, Dena, Nelson, Helena, Billy, Kenny, and many others 2 many to name. I also have unformally adopted an orphaned young black male named Mootaw who lives at my house in Atlanta. I have given my friends Benz' (300 CE) brand new and all kinds of jewelry. I've given my sister the deed 2 my house (cuz she was pregnant) and covered all prenatal care 4 her and my cousin as well as all other bills and things. I've bought my mom's and aunt cars as well as my uncle and cousins. That's just my nature 2 give all that I can 2 those that I love. I've given bums 100 dollar bills and strangers have been treated 2 dinner at 4 star restaurants on numerous occasions. I'm not a trick I'm just good hearted and believe in sharing, that's the good side now on my flip side I'm no joke. I can be cold hearted, merciless and relentless in my pursuit of revenge when pushed 2 the point. But I only strike out in self defense. I have <u>never</u> harmed anyone or anything unless they were meaning 2 do me harm first. I'm honest almost to a fault. I say exactly what I feel sometimes without thinking of the outcome (as you have seen). So in a nutshell that's my personality. Mix in a little mischief, passion, intelligence and sensitivity and you can almost feel me! Next!

HEALTH: After getting shot I started 2 workout a little but before that I didn't do shit. No weights, no pushups, nothing. I eat like an animal but can't seem 2 gain more than 165 pounds (go figure!) I eat pork (don't tell nobody ☺ And I love RIBS. Besides all of that I'm healthy thank God. Before getting shot I've never been sick or even had a cold. I've been lucky. Sexually I've never been given a sexually transmitted disease and I have never passed one on either ☺. I have been tested 4 aids (since the shooting) and I am negative. I have perfect vision, I run fast, I love hard and I don't snore ☺ Next!

~~MEN~~ I MEAN WOMEN ☺: I LOVE BEAUTIFUL WOMEN. From the curve in their backs to the length of their nails. I love the little things as much as the big ones. I love lingerie, slow kisses, passionate lovemaking and romantic dinners. I CAN COOK better than most women (including my mother and aunt) and I enjoy cooking 4 that special someone but that's a treat. I like the breasts of a woman the most, then her hair and nails. The mouth is very important to me almost as major as the eyes. I love eyes and deep eye contact. My favorite trait of a woman is her voice. The sweetness and softness of her tone and of course a sense of humor that's very important. Like u said the chemistry is infinite but once I feel it it's on 4 real! Next!

RELATIONSHIPS: Here's where I may lose u.

Whether we're friends, fuck buddies (as you so frankly put it) or man and woman (I'm too old 2 be anybody's boyfriend ☺) it has to be intense. 2 be honest I have never had just a friend or just a lover or just a woman. I want all three in one. I'm very greedy but not overimposing. I believe in the old fashioned system. There can only be one dominant presence in a relationship at least as far as masculinity goes and that's for a man. My woman should make me her priority and love me with every drop of spit in her mouth no exceptions. Without passion I become bored so there must be a constant elevation of intensity between us. There can be no secrets between her and I. The only time I should be unsure of her next move is in bed. I give a lot to my relationships I have sometimes been known to give too much but it's only because I love deeply not in pieces and bits. I have been in love but never have I stayed in love. Women tend to relax when they feel they "have" me and shit breaks down. I'm big on communication from our hopes and dreams to the position you prefer in bed. (I'll get into that in the sex section) 2 me every relationship is both a lesson and a journey unique in every way. Next!

LOVE: This one is difficult.

I can fall in love in a matter of days and on the other hand it can take years b4 I truly love someone. It depends on the intensity factor. A woman has to conquer my heart, mind and body (in that order) b4 I can truly say I love her but once done it's hard 2 fall out of love unless she was pretending or being false in some way, I can love a woman 4 many reasons. Maybe 4 what I can give 2 her or make her into or even vice versa 4 what she can make me into or share with me. I have loved young ghetto girls and older rich girls all in different ways. As far as my ideal woman. I'm not too sure. First of all she must be faithful in every way. Not just with her body but faithful in the sense that regardless of where she is or who she's with she must represent me in the utmost. She has to be woman enough to allow me 2 control our situation in public it is disrespectful 2 me 2 c a woman arguing with a man while she with her man. Feel me? Not my slave but my partner. There can only be one driver in the car. When a woman allows her man to represent her in public it shows other men her satisfaction and respect 4 her man. Let's say 4 example we're at dinner and the waiter brings you the wrong meal, instead of you dealing with it, your man handles the situation 4 u. Feel me? On the other hand suppose we're out and a guy comes on 2 u. Instead of the man intervening, it is on the woman 2 put the man in place in a sweet way sparring his feelings. This shows security in the relationship. Basically, I dislike loud women or jealous women it's a major turn off. My women has 2 understand in my profession women come at me constantly. If she's secure there's no need 2 be rude or selfish she should be happy I am loved by so many this is my business and it affects not just me but us as a couple. This part is deep but hopefully u get the drift if not I'll explain it in depth in a separate letter. Next!

SEX! (This is where the fun starts)

4 me sex is deep and mental. It's much more than in and out, up and down, bump & grind. Foreplay is the foundation for pleasurable love making. The kiss tells it all. I love 2 kiss not just on the mouth but the entire body. The elbows, the back of the knees, the neck, the ears, the breasts and every inch in between. Variety is the major part. I like 2 make love on the bed, in the kitchen, in the shower, on the floor wherever the passion moves us. I like 2 do it slow but I change speeds with the intensity. Positions help to bring pleasure in ways no one can imagine, but even before intercourse I like to tease the woman with my dick (excuse my French) barely slipping it in and then pulling it out. I like to use my tongue 2 explore her whole body prolonging the act to the point of torture. Anticipation brings ecstasy! I like to hold the woman throughout the entire act, sometimes firmly and at the other times softly. I like 2 use ice, honey, whip cream, cucumbers, anything 2 add variety, blindfolds and soft ropes are exciting. As well as cough drops and ice cream. I like 2 be dominant and submissive. Loud and quiet. When making love the Gemini comes out of me I can be gently making love in one moment and passionately fucking your brains out in the next. I love getting kissed on my neck licked on my chest and sucked well . . . you know what I mean. Basically as you can see I'm deep into making love. I like quickies as well as long passionate sessions of love making like I said variety is the key. Well now that I'm all sweaty and horny let's move on! ☺

Turn the page this page is hot as hell ☺

You alright? Hope I didn't scare you away. You must be like "Damn this nigga is a stone cold freak!" Well your half right (I'm not cold at all ☺) Anyway back 2 u. That's enough of me and what I like. I read what you asked of me in your last letter, (your favor) well it's done! Each and every night you'll get that moment. I keep trying 2 tell my-self not 2 speak of sex in my letters and in the future I'll do less of that, that's a promise! Now do me a favor. The next time your out with your "friends", out of nowhere tell 'em 2PAC said hi and let me know their response. It has 2 be when they don't expect it. Can u do that 4 me? Please? I got all your pictures in my locker bringing sunshine 2 my dreary cell but like I said "I'm greedy", so send more when u can. Remember variety is the key! I think I cov-ered the profile part. By the way u will never know the sensations I got when you called me "Boo" in your last let-ter (whew) ☺! Be careful in the kitchen love don't burn the spot down before I get to see it. Oh u asked me what my 5 year plan was so here it is!

IN 5 YEARS I WANT TO RULE THE WORLD!

Is that too much? Seriously, I want to write, act and di-rect my own movies, I want to write, produce and perform my own albums (completed) I want to manage and pro-duce other groups (completed) I also want to establish a youth program called "US FIRST" and build and run a center called "GHETTO HEAVEN" and put out a magazine called "GHETTO GOSPEL" at the same time open a restau-rant, buy another house, another BMW, and find a woman 2 be my queen in this kingdom I will build. Is that 2 much? I'm already half way finished with most of this and the rest is in the works upon my release. SHIT DON'T STOP! The world is OURS! In my next letter I'll explain my youth program 2 U. I remember you said "It's all about the youth" ☺ Keep ya head up. Keep me in your heart & mind and never sleep until you've thought of us together. Promise Me! Sleep good tonight! I miss you Ms. Angela "Lovely" Ardis.

ETERNALLY,
Tupac Amaru Shakur (signed)

My real name!
Who could make
This up! ☺

Tupac Amaru Shakur
6-16-71

Constantly Thinking of U!

I'd just started writing my letter when Tanya threw one of those fabulous gossip papers at me.

"Did you read this?" she asked.

"No, what?"

"He's writing you love poems, and he's supposed to be marrying Jada Pinkett. See, I told you they ain't no good."

"It's gossip, Tan. Half of this stuff ain't even true."

"Yeah, well, the other half is, so you figure out which half this article falls under," she said as she closed the bathroom door.

"He said he had a special friend besides me. He doesn't owe me anything anyway, Tan."

The door flew open. "No, he doesn't. But if he's truly marrying her, then he owes her something," she said, closing the door again.

"I'll ask him," I said, a bit let down. I heard the spray can being emptied behind the bathroom door.

Dear Tupac,

I'm so happy that you finally got all of my other letters. I hope you got the pictures, too. Since you gave me such a thorough breakdown, I wrote one for you.

Personality: I am a "sometimey" kind of person. I don't do anything all of the time, so I would have to say that I'm unpredictable. Most people would call me moody. The only time I come close to that word is when someone is attempting to take me for granted or when I'm in business mode. I'm extremely verbal and very hard to intimidate. I don't kiss ass, suck up, or say things I don't mean. I am excruciatingly honest if you ask for my opinion. I've hurt people's feelings on more than one occasion because I was so blatant. But I always say, "Don't ask me if you don't want my opinion." For the most part, I'm very good-natured, very silly—no, extremely silly—almost childlike at times. Everyone I meet doesn't get to see that side of me. It depends on my mood at the time and on what the particular person inspires within me. When I'm serious, I'm serious, and there isn't a lot in life that I take seriously. Just don't mess with my money or my momma, and the monster from within will never surface. I'm loyal to a select few, and love my momma to death. I tend to be nice to everyone, unless you rub me the wrong way, but even then I will be polite. I can be as timid as a mouse and I can also be a ball buster if I have to. I'll do almost anything once, and twice if I like it ☺. I'm a giver at heart and love to see people smile from the inside.

Health: I'm healthy. I work out three to four times a week and hate every minute of it. If I could blink it away, I would. Hips run in my family. I eat whatever I want, making no stipulations on meals. Life, to me, is too short not to indulge! I deny myself nothing!!!!!

Men: I love men who smell good, have nice teeth, and take care of themselves. I like ones who are professional and those with a definite edge. I don't appreciate knuckleheads, hardheads, or drama kings. I don't like needy men, clingers, or insecure men. I'm not controllable, so those kind get on my nerves, too. I like aggressiveness, but not forcefulness; romantic men but not overbearing men; accommodating men but not yes men. I like the ones who have an edge, ones who can dress up or down and fit in anywhere. He can speak well but slang at the same time, and he is secure with himself and his goals. But I don't have a type at all. I do have a preference for dark chocolate men, but that's only a preference. It's a chemistry thing.

Relationships: I don't know whether to give you my ideal one or the ones I've had. I'll give you both. My ideal relationship is one of sheer love. I believe that if a man truly loves you and you truly love him, then everything else will automatically be there. We'll respect each other, show adoration, have strong trust, enjoy flowing communication, have a good time together, and enjoy a solid relationship. But I also feel that two people must love and know themselves because if they don't, they can't truly love each other fully. I give a lot in my relationships. I can give you only what you motivate and inspire me to give to you by your energy. Every guy doesn't get the same person from me. It depends. You feel me? I've been blinded by bullshit, but I will try everything I can before throwing in the towel. Once I throw in the towel, I can't take it back. I can still be cool with an ex, but he'll never be my man again. I believe I can love you that fully and thoroughly only one time because after that, there's negative history present that will always sabotage the possibility of a clean slate. In my book, every guy I date starts out with a clean slate. I try not to carry old baggage into new relationships. It's not fair, so I release the negative as an experience and move on. Sometimes. I do agree with you in regards to people getting comfortable. I always tell guys, "You presented yourself in a way that got my attention and interest, now how long you hold that interest is up to you." I don't like perpetrators who try to impress me. I never want to meet your representative. I want to meet the man you truly are, and I'll give you the same. Realness. Just be real.

Love: I love the thought of love. I love the feeling of giving love. Real love. But because I give love so unconditionally and so freely, I tend to get smashed a lot, or rather, taken for granted. Certain people have made me feel so extremely bubbly that I want to do everything for them. When I love you, whenever I see a need I try to fill it. But I have realized that people don't know what to do with my kind of love. It's taken for granted instead of fully appreciated. I tend to find either those who can show me but not tell me or those who can tell me but not show me. Rarely do I find someone who can do both. In terms of being in love? My take on that is that depending on the day, I can be in love with you. It depends on the circumstances of the day and how we were together and our communication level and the foreplay throughout the day (which may or may not lead to sex). If everything is clicking, then that may be a day that I feel like I'm in love with you. Don't get me wrong. I will love you in general very much, but being *in love* is a day-to-day thing for me. Maybe I just haven't found the right person yet. I love hard and fully.

Sex: I love the *thought* of sex. Soft, romantic sex; passionate, aggressive sex; and maddening, rapelike sex (minus the abuse ☺). My ideals of sex sometimes block me from actually enjoying the process of it. I *love* foreplay, when a man is truly interested in pleasing me. Women can tell the difference. Foreplay can be aggressive, as long as it's not marking me or is extremely ☺ painful. It can also be gentle and slow, as long as the man doesn't have a feather hand. I hate that. I won't break. I like kissing, love kissing, adore kissing, as well as sucking, licking, biting, clawing, soft scratching, light to medium choking, hair pulling, sweaty sex ☺! If the foreplay isn't real, then the initial insertion won't be fulfilling. Don't get me wrong. It might be great sex, but for me, "mind-boggling sex" is a package thing, not just a hard dick thing. You feel me? *Teasing during sex drives me crazy!!!!!!!!!!!!!* I love that, too ☺. My favorite spot—what gets me without fail—is when my lover comes from behind me, slides his hands around me, massaging my breasts and kissing, licking, and sucking my neck and ears. It's the best!!!!!!!!!!!!! Whew, let me cool off for a minute . . .

Okay, I'm back! ☺. I like a man who's not in a hurry, who truly knows how to dominate me to the point where I'm asking for it. Anyway, I enjoy being the aggressor. I find that men like women who can dominate and be aggressive in bed. Men will mumble, plead, groan, breathe deeply, and even beg. It's a wonderful thing. It's up to me at that point whether I want to give it to them or not. My choice. What a powerful thing that is. You feel me? But I think the key to my G-spot is mental sexing, followed by intense, moderately aggressive foreplay, followed by deep, passionate sex. I'm in touch with myself enough to please myself when needed. I also enjoy the extras like toys, handcuffs, wax, ice, etc. ☺

Now I'm horny. Let's move on!!

Goals: My five-year goal is simply to be happy no matter what I do. Whether I'm still working at my current job (which I doubt), modeling, writing, whatever, I just want to be happy. I'd wanted to be a *Jet* Beauty of the Week since I was young. I did that. I wanted to be in *Playboy*. I did that. I'd like to ride the covers of magazines, sign with a makeup line, get a book published, and maybe try acting. Who knows? But all in all, I just want to be happy!

There is my breakdown for you. Oh! I did what you asked. In one of your letters, you told me to tell everyone that you said hello. They looked at me like I was crazy. I explained the story and needless to say, they were surprised. The guys said to "tell Pac to stay strong," "tell him he was framed— that was some bullshit," "tell him we got his back." It was mad love for you. But it's all good. You probably get love like that all the time. All in all, they said, "What's up?" ☺

Well, that's that, Boo. Oh, yeah. I was reading one of life's most infamous trash papers. So you and Jada are getting married, huh? Are you two having kids any time soon? It's trash, but it comes from somewhere. So, what's up with that? Is she the friend you were talking about? Care to share?

Get at me!
Forever,
Angela

P.S. I'm lovin your CD!

Jada had to be the friend he was talking about. It was the thought of them getting married. Why was it important to him that I find a star at midnight? Why was it important that I promise him I wouldn't sleep until I thought of us together? He was engaged. What in the hell was that all about?

"I've been talking to you for less than a month, and instead of just telling me you're engaged, you decide to tell me she's only a friend?"

"You don't understand," he said, defending himself.

"I understand, Pac. You're walking the man's tightrope."

"The what?" He looked confused.

"You're not ready to pick a side yet, so by staying on the rope, in your mind, you're safe."

"It's not about being safe . . ."

"You want me to open up to you and treat you like the boyfriend I trust, but you're not holding up your end with this kind of mess." I threw the paper at him. He looked down at it and laughed.

"C'mon, Ms. Lovely. It's not what you think," he said, grabbing me from behind. A slight but definite smile separated my lips at his touch.

"Men always say that so that the woman looks like she's trippin'."

"Shhh." He turned me around to face him, but I turned my head away, not wanting to look at him.

"It ain't cool, Pac, and this isn't going to make it better."

He placed his finger over my lips. "Angela," he said, but I wouldn't look at him.

"Angela," he said again, turning my face to his. I could feel the heat of his breath on my lips. He looked at me quietly, reassuringly. "Angela."

"Angela! Hello!" Tanya called out. "Are we going to lunch or what?"

I looked slowly away from the window and up at her in disgust.

"What did I do?" she asked, taken aback by my look.

I took a deep breath, grabbed my purse, and walked past her.

"What? What did I do?"

I could hear her trailing behind me.

Chapter 9

TRYING TO GET TO THE BOTTOM OF IT

Tupac Shakur # 95A1140
CLINTON CORRECTIONAL FACILITY
P O BOX 2001
DANNEMORA N Y 12929

E-5-16

CLINTON
CORRECTIONAL
FACILITY

M.S. Angela Lovely Ardis
1404 Summit Springs Drive
Dunwoody, GA. 30050

Angela,

No I am not marrying Jada. It was never an issue. Yes she did ~~ask~~ ask me but it was more out of pity than real love. Don't get me wrong I DO LOVE JADA but only as a friend. We've been through alot together. No, I have never had physical relations with her JUST friendship in it's purest form. Please know I am trying my hardest 2 be honest with U even when it's not what U want 2 hear. In my first letter I told U about the person in my life didn't I? Well here's more information on her. Her name is Keisha. We've been real with each other and seeing each other 9 9 months on the 19 of March. I've cheated on her, got shot up, and basically drug her through hell but she's stayed in my corner and I am very loyal so she's the special person in my life. I now have a real good relationship with her. We have no secrets. She knows of U but not your name. I just told her I had an intense pen pal in GA. and one day we'd meet. She's not my girlfriend but I am her King and I consider her 2 be my Queen. I have written her poetry but I have not written any of the poem made for U & her that's my word. It's not in me 2 be dishonest & shady. I don't tell her the same things I tell U and vice versa. She knows that I like U and I'm attracted 2 U and she's jealous but she also knows she's my Queen and jealousy is not becoming of a Queen. She's real cool. I say all this 2 say if by chance I was ever 2 be married ~~real fast~~ it would be her, not Jada. Now, I'm sure you are through with me at this point but I only went into detail because of your questions about Jada. She (Keisha) really has nothing 2 do with U or U with her but I wanted 2 keep everything clear. So where does that leave us, U ask? Exactly where we are. Nothing changes. We have just met and we are growing everyday And if I had known U 4 9 months I'm sure things would have been different but such is life. I can feel U right now. Your mind racing a mile a minute, hating me, feelings hurt, changing, but I hope after all of that u C I'm being what most niggaz can't be honest. I'm doing what people promise to do but fail to do. Keep it Real. If U & I had been through heaven and hell 4 nine months and then I was attracted 2 someone else what would u want? Be honest! I Love Keisha but I'm attracted 2 u and was and am curious 2 C what will become of our words and wishes. Can u feel me !? what R U thinking. In all my years I have learned a few things from women and one thing I noticed is they pray 4 honest men but find it hard 2 accept the truth when it's dealt to them. Plus you know how selfish some women can be 😊 You would not believe how deep I can feel u right now I am anticipating your reactions B4 u have them and it doesn't look good 4 me but in my eyes only sparks burn out true fires burn eternally. I want 2 be an honest and honorable man regardless of the consequences I may face. Where do we go from here? Is this the end of our Road. Will u cease 2 think of me? Will u ignore My star at midnight? Will u write me less or not at all? Will u just walk away and look elsewhere, or will u still just go through the motions just to seem nonchalant and not be sincere or whole hearted? If u wish all of these are options. But here's another option. Look at this like "Damn I have yet 2 meet a nigga this real" who when everything was going good he told the truth not when caught but when it was needed. A nigga who doesn't use women and throw them away when he's finished. A loyal man who says what he means and means what he says. Someone who truly loves for life not just when he's inside of me, or when things are good. Where are all the good men? U decide! Don't change on me Angela it would upset me and prove that Honesty

outdated and overrated. I meant every word I wrote u
That's my word. Do what u MUST. I'll keep the faith.

STILL!

2PAC

Tupac C.K.

P.S. WHERE R MY BiKiNi pictures MS. lovely?

Am I ass out Now 🙂

Angela,

No. I am not marrying Jada. It was never an issue. Yes she did ask me but it was more out of pity than real love. Don't get me wrong I do love Jada but only as a friend. We've been through a lot together. No, I have never had physical relations with her just friendship in its purest form. Please know I am trying my hardest 2 be honest with you even when it's not what u want 2 hear. In my first letter I told u about the person in my life didn't I? Well here's more information on her. Her name is Keisha we've been real with each other and seeing each other 4 9 months on the 19 of March. I've cheated on her, got shot up, and basically drug her through hell but she's stayed in my corner and I am very loyal so she's the special person in my life. I now have a real good relationship with her. We have no secrets she knowz of u but not your name. I just told her I had an intense pen pal in GA and one day we'd meet. She's not my girlfriend but I am her King and I consider her 2 be my Queen. I have written her poetry but I have not written any of the poems made for u 4 her. That's my word. It's not in me to be dishonest & shady. I don't tell her the same things I tell u and vice versa. She knows that I like u and I'm attracted 2 u and she's jealous but she also knows she's my Queen and jealousy is not becoming of a Queen. She's real cool. I say all this 2 say if by chance I was ever to be married real fast it would be to her not Jada. Now, I'm sure you are through with me at this point but I only went into detail because of your questions about Jada. She (Keisha) really has nothing 2 do with u or u with her but I wanted 2 keep everything clear. So where does that leave us u ask? Exactly where we are. Nothing changes. We have just met and we are growing everyday and if I had known u 4 9 months I'm sure things would have been different but such is life. I can feel you right now. Your mind racing a mile a minute, hating me, feeling hurt, changing, but I hope after all of that u c I'm being what most niggaz can't be honest. I'm doing what people promise to do but fail to do. Keep it real. If u & I had been through heaven and hell 4 nine months and then I was attracted 2 someone else what would u want? Be honest! I love Keisha but I'm attracted 2 u and was and am curious 2 c what will become of our words and wishes. Can u feel me!? What r u thinking. In all my years I have learned a few things from women and one thing I noticed is they pray 4 honest men but find it hard 2 accept the truth when it's dealt to them. Plus you know how selfish some women can be ☺. You would not believe how deep I can feel u right now. I am anticipating your reactions b4 u have them and it doesn't look good 4 me but in my eyes only sparks burn out true fires burn eternally. I want 2 be an honest and honorable man regardless of the consequences I may face. Where do we go from here? Is this the end of our road? Will u cease 2 think of me? Will u ignore my star at midnight? Will u write me less or not at all? Will u just walk away and look elsewhere, or will u still just go through the motions just to seem nonchalant and not be sincere or whole hearted? If u wish all of these are options. But here's another option. Look at this like "Damn I have yet to meet a nigga this real" who when everything was going good he told the truth not when caught but when it was needed. A nigga who doesn't use women and throw them away when he's finished. A loyal man who says what he means and means what he says. Someone who truly loves for life not just when he's inside of me or when things are good. Where are all the good men? U decide! Don't change on me Angela it would upset me and prove that honesty is outdated and overrated. I meant every word I wrote u that's my word. Do what u must. I'll keep the faith.

STILL!
2PAC (signed)
Tupac A Shakur (signed)

P.S. Where R my bikini pictures Ms. Lovely?
Am I ass out now ☺

Pac,

Hey, I got your letter, and once again, I truly appreciate your honesty. But . . . you are such a Gemini! ☺ Such a contradiction. And it sounds like a double standard within your relationship with Keisha. Not that it's any of my business, but you shared, so I'll indulge. How can you *honestly* tell a female who is your "Queen" about another woman and not expect jealousy? Especially after you've already "cheated" on her, as you put it. That's not very realistic. She's human and so are you, but your love quotient is not typical. Therefore, I would have to conclude that the love you share with her is anything but typical. I'd bet that you couldn't handle the situation if it were reversed! Men kill me with that double-standard shit! You claim you don't like jealous women, but you're damn near breeding insecurities into Keisha with your actions. Because, as you said before, if you weren't where you are now, you would have broken your promise in weeks, and what would that have been like for Keisha? She must truly be a special case to be able to deal with your level of love. I wouldn't be so understanding. You would already have a headache from me. I've been cheated on. I don't know too many women who haven't been. And I swear that when I find out (because we always find out), I become another person, and "jealousy" doesn't begin to describe the wrath that takes over ☺. I guess I commend her, as long as she's happy within herself and not just caught up on the fact that she's with you. She's the only one who truly knows. But what do you really expect her to say? "Oh, baby, okay. Once again, you go ahead and see where this goes, and I'll be here for you always." Come on, man. Where's the reality in it all? She will get tired of your bullshit eventually, too, I think! She's real cool, you said. But don't take advantage of that coolness. Don't take her for granted. Then men wonder why women are so tainted. It's because they sit around and allow themselves to be consumed with such great levels of bullshit from men. This is not a blame to men, just an insight into females' tainted psyches. However, this is just my mind processing your situation. I guess you two have somewhat of an understanding. If you two are content with this, then who am I to be concerned? I just don't want to hurt anyone's feelings, now that I know she's more important than a friend. She's a "Queen," your queen, and I'm a friendly curiosity ☺. So be it, Pac. Thank you for the extensive knowledge of her and ya'll's understood relationship.

And no, I wouldn't say I was hating you at all, but my mind was racing a mile a minute. This huge stop sign popped up. If I had been through heaven and hell with you for 9 months and then you were attracted to someone else, I would expect you to contain yourself, just as you would if the tables were turned. If you're honestly trying to be with me, on the real, I would expect exclusivity. Do you think she doesn't get attracted to other guys? I'm sure she gets attracted, too, but I bet she doesn't indulge. It's fine to look, to flirt (in moderation), and to fantasize, but when the line is crossed and the reality is no longer blurry, what do you really have with someone? What is the basis of the relationship, per se? But then again, you did use the word "friend," which is a noncommittal word. But "Queen" puts it somewhere else, doesn't it?

You know, women do pray for honest men, Pac. But it doesn't make it okay to tamper with emotions. Women get so emotionally involved when they love. So if you're bouncing from attraction to attraction, that's affecting her emotions on the foulest of levels. But since I know that everything has two sides and there are two of you involved—and, like I said before, as long as she's happy—cool. And as long as you're happy, cool.

Where do we go from here, you ask? On the exact path we've been on. Nothing changes. This is not the end of the road, and midnight will continue to be yours. My letters will flow freely, and my emotions will remain sincere and whole-hearted. Just keep it real, and it will always be all good.

I've enclosed your bikini shots. Hope you like 'em.

Love,
Angela

P.S. You're not ass out, Tupac! It's all good.

Feel Me

(Written exclusively for Tupac Shakur from Angela Ardis)

Baby I can feel you as I go through my day
Your mind is calling me trying to get in touch with me from so far
away
I'm reaching out for you, wanting to hold you, trying to embrace
That person inside you, trying to hide you, who hasn't found his
face

Can you feel what I'm saying? Is the sincerity clear?
Should I slow down so that you can catch up, you have no need to
fear
My intentions are harmless but as real as it will get
I won't hurt you, won't desert you, I've not even begun yet . . .

To show you what I think you need the one thing you've never had
A shoulder to lean on someone to cry to when things get real bad

Judgmental I am not, tears are a cleansing of the soul
When life gets too stressful and it begins to take its toll . . .

On your mind, on your body, it consumes your every thought
I want to be there for you, confide in me, I'm the person that's been
sought
Out by God for you Tupac and our Destiny is quite clear
Fear me not, fear me not, baby have no fear!

I can feel you Tupac and I hope you can feel me too
I'm in your heart, in your mind, there's nothing you can do
I'm here for a reason no one can tell me why
But it's not important because we have a special tie . . .

That is quite confusing and as odd as it seems
You consume my days and my nights with beautiful dreams
Of a friend ☺ I can trust and a person to whom I can confide
With no inhibitions, no hesitations, I have nothing to hide

Can you feel me my love? Am I getting my point across?
If not then this poem is a total loss
Of words that mean nothing and feelings not well expressed
Which means that this poem would be considered one big mess ☺

Feel me baby, let me know you're there
Embrace my words and let me feel that you care
Can you do that for me or is it too much to ask for?
Feel me now? Pick up your pen and write till your hand is sore. ☺

"So much for anything long-term," I said, turning over on my stomach.

"What makes you say that?" Tupac responded, rubbing my back.

"Well, you have your queen, and even though you've said each day we grow . . . well, the same goes for you two, which means there is no catchup point. You'll get deeper with her and me at the same time, and then what? Someone will eventually have to be cut off," I said, my words muffled in the pillow.

"Baby, why are you worried about that now? I'm here with you," he said, smiling.

"Oh, that makes everything okay. I feel better now. And tomorrow you'll be somewhere with her. I don't share very well," I said, looking at him.

"You don't have to."

"What do you mean?" I said, as he turned me on my back and slid on top of me.

"Trust me," he whispered in my ear. My eyes closed as chills ran over my body. I could feel him, his warmth, his wanting, and I shifted to accommodate.

"Take your clothes off," he whispered, kissing my shoulder.

"I can't. My mind is inside your letter," I gasped.

"Look at me," he said, as his face hovered over mine.

I was inside his eyes, and my entire body swelled at the thought of his tongue exploring my mouth. He began his descent, and I parted my lips in preparation for what I knew was coming. He brushed my lips with his, and his hands rested inside my hands above my head.

"I'm not a double standard, Angela. I'm just a man," he whispered.

"Gosh darn double standards!" Tanya yelled.

I snapped to and was a bit disoriented. I gave her that look again, but she ignored me this time.

"I know you don't agree with this!" she said.

I gave her a once-over and smiled slowly. "Inhale through your nose and blow out through your mouth. Just inhale and blow it out your mouth, girl."

Chapter 10

AN INVITATION

For me, the splendor of the gym was the massage I got once a week and the steam bath with which I rewarded myself after every workout. It was my quiet time away from work, away from drama, away from everything. It gave me time to meditate and to clear my head of all things irrelevant. As my sweat merged with the moisture the steam provided, I closed my eyes and exhaled, freeing my mind once again.

"At least being on the water lends a faint breeze. God, it's hot today!" I yelled, wiping the sweat from my brow.

"Here, baby, let me help you with that," Tupac said, coming up from below in the boat with an ice pail in one hand and two champagne glasses in the other. My eyes met his, and he sat on the lounge chair beside me. He dipped his entire hand inside the ice bucket for several seconds, then placed it slowly on my chest. The humidity from my body heat and the coolness of his hand provided cool air around my face. He lowered

my lounge chair, and I turned over on my stomach. I closed my eyes, listening to the ice making room for his hand as it descended into the pail once again. Undoing my bikini top, he placed both ice-cold hands on my back. His hands began tracing the curve of my spine down to the rise of my butt, down my thighs, to the bottoms of my feet. My temperature decreased considerably as he blew soft breaths over my chilled body. I exhaled again and again, trying to get a hint of cool air into my lungs, but it was so hot, almost suffocating.

"Are you okay?" Tupac asked urgently as I gasped for air. "You okay?"

"Are you okay?" I heard someone say. I had been taken out of the steam room and was sitting upright on the cold tile floor right outside the door.

"What happened?" I asked, confused, noticing about four strangers hovering over me.

"You had your face turned toward the steam spouts, and I guess when the steam came on, you couldn't breathe," an older lady explained matter-of-factly. "Here, let us help you up, sweetie." Two of the ladies took my arms and assisted me to my feet.

"I'm fine," I assured them. "No more falling asleep in there, huh?" I joked.

"At least, not right across from the steam spouts," they said, laughing, and dispersed. I found my way to my locker, finished the water in my bottle, and just sat still for what seemed like an hour but was really a little over twenty minutes. I could hear my pager buzzing and my cell phone beeping. I had a couple of guesses who it probably was and knew there was no immediate urgency to returning either of the phone calls. I slowly pulled on my sweats and made my way out of the gym and into the warm night air.

I could hear my phone ringing as I opened the door to the apartment. My legs were pretty sore from my workout, but I ran to my room and caught the phone on the fourth ring.

"Hello," I said, breathing heavily. I could hear laughter on the other end.

"Did I catch you at a bad time? If I did, I'm jealous," he joked. I smiled at the fact that it was Tupac.

"No, you didn't catch me at a bad time. I just got in from the gym. How are you?" I crooned.

"I'm cool," he responded softly. "I tried to call you earlier, but you weren't home and I didn't want to leave a message this time," he said.

"I'm glad you called back."

"I thought I'd give it another try. I wanted to see if it would be okay if my cousin contacted you so that ya'll can talk about when you would be able to come up here," he said hesitantly. I was surprised.

"That was fast, huh?" I said as he laughed.

"I know it's sooner than we had anticipated, but I can't wait. I want to meet you," he said.

I couldn't help but laugh. He had this way of saying things that was adorable and childlike.

"Yeah, Pac, that would be cool. I really want to meet you, too. Just let him know around what time to call, or he can just leave a message and I'll call him back."

"Cool. Did you have a good day?" he asked.

"It was all right. How 'bout yours?"

"Please. Every day in here is hell," he said matter-of-factly.

"I'm sorry. You're right. That was a stupid question," I said, feeling bad that I'd even asked it.

"Don't worry about it. I'll just go read one of your poems, sniff your envelope, and kiss your picture, and my night will be filled with a lot more pleasant thoughts than my day has been," he said. We laughed. "I have to go, but my cousin should be calling you soon."

"Okay," I said.

"Good night," he said softly.

"Good night," I whispered, and we hung up.

I realized that getting calls from Tupac was weird when I actually stopped long enough to think about it. It was nice, though— a cool surprise from time to time. I took a shower to wash my workout down the drain. As I slipped into my pajamas, my phone rang.

"Hello," I said.

"Hi, baby. How was your day?" my mom asked.

"It was okay. Work was hectic, my workout was torture, and Tupac called," I said in a rush.

"What was he talking about?" she asked.

"He just wanted to know if it would be all right with me if he gave his cousin my phone number to discuss when I was going to go up there," I said hesitantly. I knew my mother. I had heard the silence that I was experiencing on the phone now so many times before. Her quiet meant so many things and encompassed a mouthful of dialogue without a word ever being spoken.

"I thought you were going to get to know him first," she said calmly.

"I am getting to know him. Don't worry. I'm not leaving tomorrow."

"Angela, you have no idea who you are dealing with. You don't know anything about Tupac, and you definitely don't know any-thing about his cousin," she replied more adamantly.

I didn't have any way of making her feel better or of erasing her worries. I really, in all honesty, didn't know what I was doing, as much as I was pretending to everyone that I did. I also knew that there was a huge potential for danger lurking.

"You're right. I don't know his cousin, and I know about Tupac only from what he's told me and from what the media says. But I'm going off of my vibes on this one and trusting my gut."

"You're trusting your curiosity, and you're hoping that it all turns out okay," she challenged.

"C'mon, Mom."

"No. You need to stop being so impulsive and think a little more before you take action on things."

"I wouldn't exactly call this being impulsive. It's being planned. Give me some credit. I'm capable of having reliable vibes just like you."

"You also have the ability to make things appear to be how you want them."

"I'm gonna be fine. I don't know how to make you more comfort-able. I guess maybe I just can't. But this is gonna happen, and it'll be fine. You told me yourself that there are no guarantees in life. Whether I wait another three months or a year, it won't matter."

"Guarantees are not promised, Angela, but the odds are not necessarily in your favor."

"Odds based on what? There are a lot of things people don't know in life and the only way they learn them is by planting their feet and digging in to see what comes out of it," I said, trying to reason with her.

"It doesn't take a lot to know what the outcome will be if you plant your feet into a field of shit instead of something solid," she retorted.

I totally understood why she was worried, but I wasn't able to justify anything that I was thinking about doing. My stomach was knotting up from this conversation.

"Mom, please. I'll be fine, and I'll keep you informed every step of the way. I promise."

She took a deep breath, and I knew the discussion was over for now.

Tanya had overheard most of my conversation from the living room, and I guess that due to the silence, she took an educated guess that I was off the phone.

"Yo mama's not too happy, huh?" she asked, standing in my bedroom doorway.

"Tan, I really don't want to talk about it right now."

I wanted to think that I was being careful and that I was being cautious and that I was thinking with a level head, but I knew I probably wasn't. I knew I was probably caught up in the entire drama and yearning for adventure. There was also a part of me that wanted a complete and well-rounded story to tell when I got older. Only, most people would not consider this to be adventurous, but rather dangerous and childish. Nevertheless, I knew I was going no matter what anyone said.

Chapter 11

THUG MANSION

few days later, I was contacted by Tupac's cousin regarding the visit.

"So you're going?" my roommate asked.

"Yes."

"I thought ya'll were going to wait a few months!"

"Well, we've changed our minds."

"But you don't even know his cousin, Ann. That's dangerous. And you're going to be in New York? If something was to happen, you don't know anyone there. Then what?" She was serious, and I knew it.

"You're right, but I'm going. And just so you know, I've already had this conversation with my mother. I've been where you're headed, so find a detour."

"Have you met his cousin yet?"

"I'm going to meet him on Saturday."

"Oh, really! Where?" she asked, scolding.

"At Thug Mansion." I smirked.

"Where? What's that?"

"Tupac's house here."

"Oh, that's safe. Does your mother know what you're doing?"

"I just told you that I already had this conversation with my mom!" I was irritated.

"But has she been updated?"

"How old am I?" I questioned, getting a little pissed. "I wasn't aware of the fact that I had to ask my mother's permission to make moves in my life," I challenged. "You know me better than that."

"Yes, I do! You're stubborn."

"No, I'm my own person! I don't live my life according to how others feel I should live it. Any mistakes I make are my own, not yours and definitely not my mother's! If this turns ugly, I have only myself to blame. And if it's a pleasant experience, I won't sit back and say I'm glad I didn't listen to Tan and Mom! I can't not go because if I didn't, I would walk around forever saying I wish I had when I could have or wondering what it would have been like. I don't and can't live my life like that. My curiosities have to be satisfied at some point, and the opportunity is knocking now. Do you understand?"

"I hear you, but . . . I don't know." She was concerned.

"I mean, Tan, you couldn't have told me a month ago that I would be writing and talking to Tupac. Now he wants to meet. Well, you couldn't have told me that either. I appreciate your concern, but I don't have any bad vibes about any of this," I explained.

"Damn a vibe. Common sense should prevail," she said in a way that thoroughly annoyed me.

"I know how I feel, and that's really all that matters. And you're not one to talk. It's not like you've always used common sense. Should I bring up some examples of when you didn't?" She rolled her eyes. "But you followed your own mind, and things turned out however they turned out, and that's that. But it was your choice! Right?" I finished, clearly expecting her to answer, but instead she smirked.

"Well, yeah, but this is different," she pleaded.

"It's not different. I'll be fine."

"Fine! Fine! Fine! Your momma's probably pulling her hair out." We looked at each other and laughed.

I understood everyone's concerns. Hell, to be honest, I was concerned myself. I am the "what-if" queen. What if something did go wrong? What if his cousin was crazy? What if Tupac was crazy? I didn't know anyone in New York; the closest people I knew were in Michigan, and Mom wasn't happy. But I didn't feel anything negative, only the normal anxieties of doing unknown things, the flurries of concern and periodic paranoia. It was going to happen. It had to happen. Damn the thought of fear that everyone was trying to instill in me. There was no place for it. I felt calm.

Early Saturday afternoon, I arrived at what was called Thug Mansion. His cousin met me outside as I parked my car in front of the house. I was expecting a mansion, but instead I found myself looking at a normal house in a middle-class neighborhood. Nothing elaborate, just a house. We went inside. It wasn't heavily furnished. I noticed just a few things in the living room as we passed and a couch in the den, where we ended up. Tupac's sister was also there and offered me something to drink. I accepted, and his cousin then asked me a few questions regarding my availability.

I sat and looked around, wondering where in the world all of Tupac's stuff was. There was one photograph of him on the wall across from me, but I didn't see anything else that made me feel even remotely that this house was associated with him. I started to think about what my mother had said and I began to have a mild anxiety attack. I was staring at his cousin's mouth moving and realized I didn't know anything about him. This might not be Thug Mansion—or his sister, for that matter. His sister handed me a glass of water, and I guess his cousin sensed something because he commented, "Tupac's stuff is in his place in New York."

"Oh," I said, smiling uncomfortably. *That makes sense*, I thought. I could see a pool through the sliding glass doors. It needed to be cleaned, but it wasn't spring yet, I rationalized. We discussed the timing of the trip, and we decided that Tupac would pay for my plane ticket and I would pay for my room and ferry. I didn't want him to pay for everything, and I didn't want to pay for everything either, so it was fair. I stayed for about an hour, then said good-bye and made my way back home. I was comfortable.

I decided to take the long way home in order to do some thinking. It was going to be a weekend thing, and I knew it would be no big deal to get that Friday off. My biggest headache would be trying to figure out what I was going to wear. It was dark when I arrived home, and Tanya was waiting impatiently on the couch.

"Hey," I said.

"So, what happened?" she asked, seeming to be holding back her excitement.

"It was cool," I said, kind of relieved that it had been. "He was cool, polite, respectful. I also met Tupac's sister, and she was cool, too."

"Was it a mansion?"

"No, it was a house, in a cul-de-sac," I said, sitting across from her.

"Was it pretty? Furnished nicely?"

"Not what one would expect, I guess. But it had a nice-sized pool in the back. I didn't go out there, but I could see it from the den area."

"Oh. So, what now?"

"Well, he's making the arrangements and will keep in touch as progress is made. When the time is here, we will go," I said, as she gave me a look. "What?"

"I admire you. As much as I bitch, I admire the fact that you always go after what you want no matter what people say or think. I wish I could do that."

"Don't wish for things you have control over. Just change them. I get scared like everyone else, but I decided a long time ago that my life is mine. I have only one. Everyone else has one, too. So if you give in to the demands and fears of others . . . well, then it's no longer yours. I don't choose to do that. No one's perfect or has all the answers. So, if I follow your mind instead of my own, what does that say about my faith in my own thought process and my own sensibilities?"

"True. True."

"I like advice, I appreciate concern, and I accept others' opinions, but the final choice regarding my actions has to be mine. And so it is and always will be," I said, getting up and going to the kitchen to get some water. She was quiet.

"So, what did you do today?" I asked, watching her from the kitchen. As she rambled on, I thought about my conclusions, the meeting, and Tupac. I believed my own hype again. I purposely set aside the possibility of any danger and thought only of the positive. Was I fooling myself?

Nope! It was all good.

> *"Well, we're alone again," he said slowly.*
>
> *"Yeah. Imagine that."*
>
> *"Are you nervous?" he asked.*
>
> *"Surprisingly, I'm not," I replied. I raised my hand to his face and slid my thumb across his cheek. He closed his eyes as he let out a low moan. His hand made its way slowly up my stomach, between my breasts, and abruptly grabbed hold of my neck. His eyes sprang open, and mine widened, as I was caught off guard. He pressed his body against mine, rubbing his lips against my earlobe. His grip was getting firmer as he moved his lips down my neck and across my cheek. I could feel his smile. My breathing became shallow as he began to slide his lips toward mine.*
>
> *The phone started to ring. As he reached the side of my mouth, he slowly said, "Answer that." I shook my head no.*

Abruptly I was thrust to the side.

"Answer it!" Tanya said, then picked it up herself, looking at me like I was crazy. We had our own phone lines, but hers was connected to the phone in the kitchen, where I was still standing. "Hello. Hold on," she told whoever it was. "What's wrong with you?

I took a deep breath, took another drink of my water, and walked slowly to my room.

"What did I do?" she asked, genuinely confused.

"Hello," I heard her say into the phone. "Oh, nothing. Sybil's back, that's all."

I ignored the comment. I would meet Tupac soon, I thought to myself. Everything was going in a forward motion. Amazing.

Chapter 12

GETTING REALLY PERSONAL

Tupac Shakur #95A1140
CLINTON CORRECTIONAL FACILITY
P O BOX 2001
DANNEMORA N Y 12929
E-5-16

Ms. Angela "Lovely" Ardis
1404 Summit Springs Dr
Dunwoody, GA. 30350

3/28/95

Dearest Angela

What'z up Love? How R U? My cuz said u 2 met and everything is in the works as far as the visit that's good. I'm very happy with how things R going 4 Us especially after reading your last letter I'm satisfied knowing that As long As I keep it real with U then It can only be positive relations between U & I. U feel me? I Believe in Destiny and everyday it becomes even more clear 2 me that our meeting is just that DESTINY! So don't look at me as your average Nigga, see me as the Nigga U were destined 2 meet! Why? Who Knows and at this point it is not important. What is very important is how we treat each other. So don't pay attention 2 outside influences (ie Mother, Media, girlfriends) Like I said picture me and treat me like the closest "girlfriend" U have ever had. Only difference is I am a man! That's a big difference but U know how it is with female & males. It's like a dick can be the barrier between true friendz and bullshit! I don't want that 4 US! I only want reality 4 us. However painful it is or Joyous it can be. It may look hopeless and uninviting right now but have No fear follow me Angela and I won't bring U grief that I can assure U. Only way 4 US 2 fail is if U lie or assume! Besides that we have a long beautiful road ahead of us. . . . Come ON, let's go!

♡ 2PAC

ANTICIPATED EC$TACY! EXCLUSIVELY

4 Angela from 2Pac
(I figure if I write it
Big U can believe me
when I tell u it's
exclusive!) ☺

Kiss me Angela, Taste my Soul
'embrace your destiny
Lay back, relax, arch your back
And leave the rest 2 me
Spread your legs but leave on the lights
So u can see my eyes
grab hold and hug while we make love
So strong it will make u cry
Tonight let's take our time it's been awhile
But there's no rush
I love the way u quiver As I Deliver
The slightest touch
My arms will take away the stress
My kiss will ease the pain
Have u ever made love that was so intense
When u came it's like falling rain
Don't blush I know u feel me
Don't be shy cuz' now's the time
Someday I'll make love 2 your physical
but tonight let me sex your mind

PASSION
& ECSTACY
2PAC

140

FOREVER INSIDE U.   4 Angela EXCLUSIVELY

from 2PAC

Was it a dream I dreamed.
last night I saw a friend who understood
The ups and downs Joy and pain
the bad as well as good
Did I fantasize or make this up
This bond I swear we have
So strong and real sometimes I feel
your so Near I can hear u laugh
There's no telling what lies at the end 4 us
Trust in me though I know your scared
But close your eyes and follow my voice
And I swear I'll guide u there
Down if I was your girlfriend or your mom u'd surely trust me
In no rush 2 touch, suck or fuck but intent on making U love me
If I don't Do Nothing I will succeed where others tried 2
Through my letters and poemz your no longer alone cuz I'll forever Be inside U

3/28/95

Dearest Angela

What's up love? How R U? My cuz said u 2 met and everything is in the works as far as the visit that's good. I'm very happy with how things are going 4 us especially after reading your last letter I'm satisfied knowing that as long as I keep it real with u then it can only be positive relations between u & I u feel me? I believe in destiny and everyday it becomes even more clear 2 me that our meeting is just that DESTINY! So don't look at me as your average nigga, see me as the nigga u were destined 2 meet! Why? Who knows and at this point it is not important. What is important is how we treat each other. So don't pay attention 2 outside influences (ie Mother, Media, girlfriends) Like I said picture me and treat me like the closest "girlfriend" u have ever had. Only difference is I am a man! That's a big difference but u know how it is with female & males. It's like a dick can be the barrier between true friendz and bullshit! I don't want that for us! I only want reality 4 us. However painful it is or joyous it can be. It may look hopeless and uninviting right now but have no fear follow me Angela and I won't bring u grief that I can assure u. Only way 4 us 2 fail is if u lie or assume! Besides that we have a long beautiful road ahead of us . .
. . . . .come on let's go!

♥ 2PAC (signed)

EXCLUSIVELY

4 Angela from 2PAC

(I figured if I write it Big u

can believe me when I tell u it's

exclusive!) ☺

ANTICIPATED EC$TACY

Kiss me Angela, Taste my soul
Embrace your destiny
Lay back, relax, arch your back
And leave the rest 2 me
Spread your legs but leave on the lights
So u can see my eyes
Grab hold and hug while we make love
So strong it will make u cry
Tonight let's take our time it's been awhile
But there's no rush
I love the way u quiver as I deliver
The slightest touch
My arms will take away the stress
My kiss will ease the pain
Have u ever made love that was so intense
When u came it's like falling rain
Don't blush I know u feel me
Don't be shy cuz now's the time
Someday I'll make love 2 your physical
But tonight let me sex your mind

PASSION
& ECSTACY
2PAC

4 Angela EXCLUSIVELY

FOREVER INSIDE U

from 2PAC

Was it a dream I dreamed
Last night I saw a friend who understood
The ups and downs joy and pain
The bad as well as good
Did I fantasize or make this up
This bond I swear we have
So strong and real sometimes I feel
Your so near I can hear u laugh
There's no telling what lies at the end 4 us
Trust me though I know your scared
But close your eyes and follow my voice
And I swear I'll guide u there
Damn if I was your girlfriend or your man u'd surely trust me
In no rush 2 touch, suck or fuck but intent on making u love me
If I don't do nothing I will succeed where others tried 2
Through my letters and poems your no longer alone cuz I'll for-
    ever be inside u

What's up, Boo?

I believe in *destiny*, too. We have been pulled together for a reason. I don't have the answers to the "whys," and I try not to dwell on the "whys" that the universe controls. I just surrender myself to whatever experience it brings me. You feel me? I want you to know that outside influences have no bearing on us. There is nothing that the media, my mother, my girlfriends, or anyone can say or do that can destroy what we're sharing. Unless, of course, we allow them to. Rest assured, it won't be me! ☺ Are you down for the long haul? ☺ I hope so.

Your poetry was tantalizing. Are you trying to seduce me? ☺ It's working. You made the first stop on our long, beautiful road. Now allow me to take you somewhere else. Come on. Let's go!!!!!!!!!!!!!!!!

STORY 1

Dusk crept into the room as their conversation continued and laughter filled the air. The closeness that they shared was from their friendship and the passion that lay hidden deep within. This evening wasn't a normal evening. The chemistry was intense, the champagne intoxicating, the music soothing, the ambiance engulfing. She sat there, hanging on every word that passed his full lips. His hands, she thought, were so strong. She imagined him touching her face, her shoulders, her breasts, her thighs, her . . .

He watched her laugh. He loved to see her laugh, so beautiful, seductive. Watching her eyes . . . the passion that danced within them was pure madness. So much to unleash, so much to explore, so much to know. *"If I could only touch her,"* he thought to himself. *"If I could show her what love should feel like. The places that that passion in her eyes could take her. If only . . ."*

The sun had gone, and they sat with the glare of the fireplace reflecting solitude. He poured more champagne and changed the CD. He smiled as he sat back on the couch.

"What are you smiling at?" she asked.

"I think you're so beautiful." He placed his hand against the side of her face, tracing the smoothness with his thumb. Her eyes closed from the warmth of his hand, and a powerful chill filled her body as her eyes slowly opened. For the first time in their relationship, they were at a loss for words. Staring into each other's eyes, they knew, at that moment, that no other words were needed . . .

They slid to the floor in front of the fireplace. He took her face in his hands and kissed her gently on her forehead, then her cheek, then her nose. Their eyes met again, and the approval for which he was searching was dancing wildly inside of hers. He kissed her passionately. She ran her hands over the back of his head and moaned. Their breathing intensified as he slowly laid her on the rug. He stared at her beneath his body and she at him . . .

"I want you," he said.

She pulled his head to her mouth as he began slowly rubbing her stomach. She exhaled as he moved to her earlobes. She began arching and squirming with every thrust of his tongue in her ear. Placing his hand under her shirt, he could feel her warm body quiver as he began caressing her breast. With her nipples hard and full of desire, she began pushing his shoulders down her body. She wanted to feel his lips on her breasts and his tongue circling around her nipples. He got right over her breasts, and she could feel the heat of his breath on her chest. He paused and got up, kneeling beside her, admiring her curves.

"What's wrong?" she asked.

"Do you trust that I would never hurt you?" he asked.

"Yes," she responded, concerned.

"Then just relax and go with the flow," he said as a grin came over his face.

Before she could say anything, he swooped over her and began kissing her passionately, while ripping her shirt open and rubbing her breasts and nipples. At first, she didn't know what to think, but found that her body was responding faster than her mind. She was wetter than she had ever been, and she never wanted anyone the way she wanted him. He was being rough but gentle. He raised and locked her hands above her head with one of his hands and began lifting her skirt. All she could think about was him inside of her, all of him, and she couldn't stand it. She flipped him over and sat on top of him. Feeling his hardness, she began to move her hips as she removed what was left of her top and bra. She ripped off his shirt. His breathing increased as she slid down his body and placed one of his nipples in her mouth. She circled her tongue, nibbling, then biting, licking, and biting again, sucking, biting, nibbling, licking. It was his turn to squirm, and he was. She loved it. She was moving on top of him to the rhythm of his squirm. He grabbed her butt and began squeezing it as she pushed down in matching motion. Her sighs where more apparent, his grasp was more firm . . .

"I want you now!" he said.

She sat up and unbuckled his pants, taking out his person. She slowly licked the head, then the shaft, and ran her tongue up and down the length of it and back to the head. Round and round she went, then she put it in her mouth and began sucking it, first softly, then hard, then softly, then harder, circling her tongue at the same time. She could see his stomach trembling and could feel his person pulsating intensely. She stopped and took her skirt off, no panties to be found. He removed his pants, laying her on the rug, teasing her with the tip of his manhood gently pressing against the opening of her vagina. She moaned, begging him to put it in. He inserted it gently, and they both exhaled. His hardness filled her with such an intensity that she gripped him as her body tightened. They rolled around the floor, thrusting and flipping each other, until they both started coming, coming, and coming, draining all their curiosities and years of pent-up passions. He held her in his arms, kissing her deeply again and again. She began thinking to herself, *"Would this feeling last? Could this feeling last? Will this friendship last? Will we remain as close as we've been? How does he feel about me now?"*

"I love you," he said quietly as he spooned her from behind.

"I love you, too," she said as she lay with him wrapped around her body, talking and watching the fire burn.

STORY 2

She ran faster and faster as the rain fell like a waterfall over her petite body. Someone was chasing her, and he wasn't that far behind. She couldn't catch her breath, so she darted down a dark alley. She couldn't hear footsteps anymore, only the pounding of her own heart.

And then, as if from nowhere, he appeared, masked and with a dark coat. She started to scream, but couldn't. He began to laugh as she tried to back away. He picked her up and threw her, face first, against the wall. She could feel his hot breath against the back of her neck. Wrapping her hair around his hand, he pulled her backward and began biting and sucking her neck and ears.

She wanted to scream, to yell, to feel anything, but what she felt was . . . very aroused. She could feel herself getting extremely wet, and regardless of what her mind was telling her, her body was in its own world. She began to squirm as he took both of her hands and pinned them against the wall with one of his. He began sliding himself up and down her body. She could feel him, all of him. He buried his face in her hair and put one of his hands on her thigh as the rain pounded their bodies. She closed her eyes and sighed to herself . . .

"Please don't hurt me," she said in a faint voice. Extreme fear and arousal raced through her veins, giving her an intense feeling in the place that was swollen with anticipation.

He said nothing. He began rubbing the inside of her thigh slowly, pressing on the back of her butt with his hardness. She let out a soft moan. He bent a little, making sure he had his entire hand cupping her vagina from front to back. She threw her head back on his shoulder as he rubbed her clitoris with his forefinger. He moved his finger back and forth, along its length, then down her thighs, back to her vagina, then used circular motions, which got harder and harder, faster and faster. She could tell his breathing had gotten harder and hotter as he grabbed her panties from the front and ripped them off, scratching her legs.

"Oh, God. Please don't hurt me! Please don't do this! Please!" she pleaded, barely audible over the pounding of the rain.

He said nothing. He didn't stop . . . she didn't want him to. He raised her skirt. She could feel his bare skin and hardness against her ass, and she shuddered with anticipation. They were soaked. Her hair stuck to her face, her clothing clung to her body. He ripped her blouse off and her breasts hung exposed. Swinging her around, he pinned her hands against the wall again and began sucking vigorously on her mounds. Her breathing was erratic. He thrust his hand into her vagina—in and out, in and out. He removed his fingers and straddled her. She could see his eyes and noticed something familiar, but just at that moment, he entered her with a powerful thrust and she cried out in ecstacy. Her body quivered and tingled like nothing she'd ever felt. He was moving in a circular motion, panting, kissing, sucking, biting her flesh. She couldn't stand it as she finally got ahold of his mask, ripped it off, and realized it was her man.

"Oh, God, yes!" she cried out as he panted and grabbed her ass in his massive hands. She thrust forward, using her strength against his shoulders, and he held her firmly in his arms, pounding, rotating, and plunging into her wet swollen nest. ☺

They climaxed simultaneously, drenched, quivering, drained, but satisfied.

"You know, if I had known this would get you off like this, I would have chased you a long time ago," he said, kissing her on her forehead as they walked home arm in arm.

Dissolve

(Written exclusively for Tupac from Ms. Lovely)

Dissolve

Shhhhh as you lay still your essence so calm
I straddle you and begin gently kneeding with my palms
My oiled hands melt from the warmth of your flesh
I lube you till you drip caressing your back with my breasts

Mmmm you moan as I place your earlobe between my lips
We move in one swift motion from the shifting of your hips
I run my hands down your sides back up to your chest
I tell you to turn over so I can do what I do best

You squirm, you flex, legs locked holding the bed
Pelvis thrusting, moans erupting inside your head
I can feel you getting closer, veins enlarged, pulsating wildly
Pulling back I just relax, hand stroking your manhood mildly

Stress dissolving, sensations linger, anticipating my next move
I descend, can't comprehend that I have something to prove
Your thoughts run freely as you get closer to your goal
Your body locks, exhale, release all that ails your soul

"Do you feel better?" I extend awaiting a word or two
You smile fully, turning me over, I now can feel you too
"It's your turn Ms. Lovely I hope you're ready to be freed,"
You strap my hands, cover my mouth as you begin to feed.

Dissolve

"I need to get some water—no, a cigarette!" Tonya screeched, laughing and fanning herself.

"Shut up!" I laughed

"Girl, I knew that you would write a letter like this. This is what he wanted."

"He started it," I defended. She threw me a look. "Okay, well, what was his last poem . . . umm . . . talking about sexing my mind?" I looked at her, anticipating something, but I didn't know what. "Well, he just got mentally sexed like I've been getting foreplay."

"Umm huh. I wonder who I could call." She looked off into the distance.

"Call for what?"

"Well, hell. I'm horny now! What am I supposed to do about it?"

"Your Mr. Mumbles is always available."

"I want some flesh. Flesh!"

"This whole situation is so different," I said, filling out the envelope.

"What's different?"

"It's mental. One hundred percent. I have never been this aroused by anyone. It's different . . . like . . . I feel like he's already touched me, and we've already hung out and talked till early morning. It's just a nice change of pace."

"I'm gonna call the jail and tell them to post a sign on the message board for a pen pal," she joked, leaving the room as if cued by the ringing of my phone.

"Hello," I said, laughing into the phone.

"Angela," he said confidently. I recognized his voice instantly.

"What's up!" I was thrilled to hear from him. "Surprise! Surprise!" I joked.

"What's up, baby? Whatchu doin'?" he asked.

"I just finished writing you and was putting together your package so I can mail it tomorrow."

"Package?"

"Yeah, man, a package filled with all kinds of goodies," I said, playing.

"What's in it?" he asked almost childlike.

"Oh, what do you think? You're the only one capable of surprises?" I joked. "Well, guess what?" I said.

"What?" he played along.

"It's a surprise!" I sung into the phone. He laughed the laugh that only he could produce, and I was filled with the knowledge that I had inspired it within him.

"Okay, that's cool. So, when will I get it?" he asked. I took an exaggerated deep breath. He laughed.

"C'mon, you can at least tell me when . . . pleeeeeeease," he begged playfully. I couldn't help but smile.

"It'll be there on Thursday. I'm going to FedEx it to you."

"Good! I can't wait to meet you."

"Me either. Soon, right?" I asked.

"Very," he said, taking a deep breath. "Damn!" he shouted.

"What's wrong?"

"I have to go, but I'll call you back soon."

"All right, Pac. Look out for this package."

"I will. And you look out for our star."

"Well, you look for me in our dark corner."

"Well, you listen for my whispers."

"If you would stop talking and stand still, my spirit would like to kiss you good night," I whispered seductively. He was quiet at first, then he chuckled to himself.

"You not right, Ms. Lovely. You fuckin' wit me. It's cool," he laughed.

"No, you'll feel like that when you get the package, Pac," I said, emphasizing his name.

"Really?" he said.

"Oh, yeah," I crooned. We both laughed. "Good night," I said.

"Yeah, all right. Good night, Angela," he said quietly, then the phone went dead.

> *"Will you just not say anything else and kiss me now?" I asked.*
>
> *"What's wrong?" Tupac asked, smiling.*
>
> *"No questions, just kisses. Just one, but it has to be now, Pac. Just kiss me now."*
>
> *"What's with all the urgency, Ms. Lovely?" he said. He softened and smiled. "Okay, Ms., come here," he said, extending his arms.*
>
> *I walked towards him. His hands grabbed my arms and pulled me close.*

"Maybe I'll just get me a pen pal overseas," Tanya said as she burst into my room and sat down on my bed. I closed my eyes, disgusted once again, but didn't bother to let her know that she had once more interrupted something potentially special.

Chapter 13

GETTING HEAVIER

Tupac Shakur #95A1140
CLINTON CORRECTIONAL FACILITY

P O BOX ___2001___

DANNEMORA N Y 12929
E-5-16

Ms. Angela "stillwely" Ardis
1404 SUMMIT SPRINGS DRIVE
Dunwoody, GA. 30350

Dearest Angela!

Damn, your last letter (or should i say package) put me in critical condition, no joke! Angela, u r absolutely no question about it drop dead gorgeous! Fuck what u heard! But enough of that I'll get back 2 the physical in a second. Your story got me heated and horny (it also gave me some ideas.) :) Put it this way u find the Alley I'll make it happen. The fireplace scene is no problem, u got that Baby! Thank 4 the variety of pictures it was a true gift! I already missed u and thought of u but now it's critical we meet. I won't be satisfied until I get to kiss the taste from your mouth. Do u mind? :) This was the best package I ever got from u. U opened up and that my love turned me all the way on! Right now I'm excited so I have 2 relax a little 2 be coherent! :) Okay where do I began Today we travel R U ready!? The first stop will be......the land of poetry Turn the page, I'll meet u there :)

①

156

I feel u

I) Whether it be your letter or picture
or the fragrance that u wear
From a distance I can feel u
There's no question that u care

II) I feel the depths of your lonliness
Your passionate moans and groans
Tonight I appeal 2 your sense of patience
It won't be long B4 I come home

III) Do u have time 4 an honest man
From whom nothing but good can come
Are U scared 2 face your destined fate
Unsure of what's 2 come

IV) I have injected my soul into your body
infecting your inner parts
seduced your mind until I find
the secrets of your heart

V) From this day forth until the end
Eternally I claim
"It's impossible 2 love a wom
until you've fucked her Brain"

4 Angela

②

157

Don't Go There!

Don't Go There!
IF u are Timid & shy, Scared 2 touch
Afraid of taking Risk
Don't follow me in the dark Because
There's passion in the mist
Such pleasure born 2 those who dare
The heavens we could share
Beware I'll steal your heart 2 get your soul if u go there

Don't go there
iF u fear the drama there in Normalcy
envious Suspicions, Inhibitions R Forever gone FROM me
This Spirit i Possess can serenade your lonely heart
Inspired by your lust if u can trust me in the dark
I'm Not Scared 2 take u there But understand the rulez of flight
There R No Secrets 2 this ride Confide and Hold me tight
our possibilities R infinite our pleasures obvious
Heaven on Earth can only be seen by a team unified in trust

2 Angela
from

③

Okay enough of the land of poetry & now back to u. We'll discuss the program (youth) when u come visit so I'll save that 4 later.

I'm glad i am in your thoughts on a regular basis that means alot 2 me and really it's very much appreciated and mutual! I C it's time 4 U & I to move up a notch huh 😊! Okay here we go we have just moved into level 2 of this unorthodox relationship! Okay enough rest! You Ready 4 fantasy land? Well what's the matter cat got ya tongue 😊 follow me 2 fantasy

FANTASY #1

Ms Angela worked hard 2day. Another day of overaggressive businesssuits and hormone crazy bosses but finally work was over and she headed home. She was having daily day dreams about her penitentiary bound pen-pal but he had at least 6 months 2 do B4 she could finally C him. So she thought about her replacements. Usually Reggie was always good 4 a fuck but lately he'd been letting his imagination of a wife & his fragile feelings get involved and that was a no-no! Reggie didn't have the heart 2 possess what she owned naturally, there was always Tim but he was a rotten lover his only saving grace was his insatiable fettish 4 eating pussy but tonight she needed more than just a tongue 2 appease the burning desire that flamed from her stomach down 2 her pink parts! she needed a complete passionate equally insatiable MAN and lately they were scarce in those parts. As she pulled up in her driveway she tried 2 decide between Tim & Reggie, maybe she could have them both shit who was she kidding between the both of them she couldn't come if she paid 4 it. She put her key in the door but it was open. She pushed the door open and cautiously walked inside. she flipped the lightswitch but no light appeared. she moved slowly 2 the livingroom 2 find a candle burning leaving the room immersed in a glow of mystery. There was a note beneath the candle:

UNDRESS AND GO TO TUB RIGHT NOW DON'T SAY A WORD OR WHISPER OR FACE EXTREME PUNISHMENT U HAVE 3 MINUTES 2 BE NAKED AND WET!

→

Quickly she made a sweeping inventory of all the lovers of her past but she could not remember one so forceful and ...... sexy! She quickly undressed and walked gracefully toward the bathroom. Her breast held firmly bouncing slightly as she entered the bathroom several candles were burning around the steaming bubble bath she slipped inside the water and for the first time noticed a walkman laying beside the tub with another note!:

U WERE 30 SECONDS LATE I WILL DEAL WITH THAT LATER. PRESS PLAY!

She pressed play and a voice instantly had her enraptured and captive. The man on the tape spoke forcifully but assuringly enticing. He spoke deeply but almost at a whisper barely audible beneath the sounds of the bubble bath. She turned up the volume His voice was deliberate and inviting as he spoke these words,

⑥

" Angela lay back and relax. let the warmth of the water bring back forgotten moments in the womb. close your eyes and use your other senses. feel the water protecting u from the cold miserable world smell the incense I have burning throughout the house, listen 2 the waves of the water as it soothes you. Listen! take your hands and place them in your hair. stroke the strands of soft hair and wet them until it hangs off of your head wipe your face of all the phoney smiles u unleashed today wipe your chest of all the stress u have stored there rub your stomach and feel the hunger for passion u possess. Now place your hands over your "life giver" and caress yourself 4 a moment. Place a finger over your clitoris and gently rub. Place another finger inside of you. Gently stroke & rub simultaneously until u feel a warm sensation in your stomach then stop and stand up "

①

As Angela followed every step in the letter she felt the stirring hunger bursting from her stomach she began 2 stand when she could smell the presence.

of a man. It was unmistakable. She then felt
two soft gentle but firm hands guide her to the
kitchen a cloth table covering was placed on the table
and she was layed out on the table on her back with
her eyes still held tightly shut. She could hear the
Fridge door opening. Then she felt the presence over
her. She felt the warm rush of his wet mouth
as he kissed her lips then her chin then
her neck up 2 her ears behind her neck
down her arms up her elbow 2 her bellybutton
up her stomach across her breast around her
hard nipples up 2 her neck over each earlobe
then back down 2 her stomach WOW! she
clinched and gripped the table as the ice
cube slid across her stomach. Using his mouth
the "presence" licked her breast from inch to inch
concentrating on the nipples. After melting the
first two she quickered as he open her legs
and placed his frigid but soft tongue into
her licking and flicking until she grabbed his
head and moaned in exstacy. He built up his
technique into a frenzied rush and had her
twitching from his touch. He pour warm honey
over her and licked as he squeezed a lemon
til it dripped on her private parts. He placed

⑧

His honey drenched finger into her vagina. She mooned at the depth of his penetration. He pulled his finger from the warmth of her essence and ordered her 2 open her mouth. She licked the man's finger and enjoyed the lemonaide tasting Ambrosia. He parted her legs further and put the head of his person into her pink parts. She clinched up and released a gasp as he slowly inserted half of his staff into her. She arched her back 2 meet the dominance of his entrance but he pulled it out mid stroke and massaged & rubbed the surrounding area of her vagina. Again he repeated his initial entrance until her moans became unbearable then he entered her fully in one merciless stroke. She clutched him in her arms like the owner of the last breath. She kissed him blindly 2 keep from yelling in passion. He rythmically stroked her in various speeds and intensities 4 at least 30 minutes before he picked her up & carried her into the livingroom he placed her on the carpet and placed her on her stomach he then put a counch pillow under he belly as he entered her from behind. He rode her with a slow controlled pace then abruptly switching 2 a wild vigorous frenzy intermittantly. He lifted her once again and lay himself on the bed and she straddled him and felt his manhood pierce her insides like a spear. She swore she could feel him entering her throat then he got up and grabbed several articles of clothing and tied her up 2 the 4 corners of the massive bed then he spoke " OPEN YOUR EYES NOW" By the time Angela opened her eyes Her penpal was already inside her stroking her like an olympic longshoremen, LONG SATISFYING complete STROKES. As she Formed her mouth 2 say his NAME He picked her up and they were standing with Her back 2 the wall with her legs in his arm as he impaled her until She Screamed his Name IN OrgASMIC INTeNSity. OH GOD 2PAC !!

See YA IN
Fantasy #2 Boo!

(10)

NEXT STOP ——————>

165

okay that's all 4 this trip. I got another favor and
I hope u do this 4 me. it's slightly crazy! okay
here's my favor. At midnite each nite until u see me
touch yourself and whisper my name 20 times.
PLEASE Angela? Would U Do that 4 me?
I Don't whose NEXT 2 U BLACK them out
and let me have some Every Night Just give
me 20 strokes and calls and I'll do the same
In time it will be real and those will be
20 of the Sweetest MOST heartfelt intense
strokes in the history of lovemaking. So please
"FRIEND" Do that 4 me. Don't go all fast I want
20 slow meaningful strokes then u can go back 2
the dud Next 2 U. He can't compare 2 this shit
we got. C ya TONITE AT Midnite LOVER!

Passionately
Cate

Dearest Angela!

Damn, your last letter (or should I say package) put me in critical condition, no joke! Angela, U R absolutely no question about it drop dead gorgeous! Fuck what U heard! But enough of that I'll get back 2 the physical in a second. Your story got me heated and horny (it also gave me some ideas) ☺. Put it this way U find the alley I'll make it happen. The fireplace scene is no problem, U got that Baby! Thanx 4 the variety of pictures it was a true gift! I already missed U and thought of U but now it's critical we meet. I won't be satisfied until I get to kiss the taste from your mouth. Do U mind? ☺ This was the best package I ever got from U. U opened up and that my love turned me all the way on! Right now I'm excited so I have 2 relax a little 2 be coherent! ☺ Okay where do I began. Today we travel R U ready!? The first stop will be . . . . . . The land of poetry turn the page, I'll meet U there ☺

I FEEL U

Whether it be your letter or picture
Or the fragrance that u wear
From a distance I can feel u
There's no question that u care

I feel the depths of your lonliness
Your passionate moans and groans
Tonight I appeal 2 your sense of patience
It won't be long B4 I come home

Do u have time 4 an honest man
From whom nothing but good can come
Are u scared 2 face your destined fate
Unsure of what's to come

I have injected my soul into your body
Infecting your inner parts
Seduced your mind until I find
The secrets of your heart

From this day forth until the end
Eternally I claim
"It's impossible 2 love a woman
until you've fucked her brain"

2PAC (Signed)
4 Angela

DON'T GO THERE!

Don't Go there!
If u are timid & shy, scared 2 touch
Afraid of taking risk
Don't follow me in the dark because
There's passion in the mist
Such pleasure born 2 those who dare
The heavens we could share
Beware I'll steal your heart 2 get your soul if U go there
Don't go there
If u fear the drama, thrive in normalcy
Envious suspicions, inhibitions R forever gone from me
This spirit I possess can serenade your lonely heart
Inspired by your lust if u can trust me in the dark
I'm not scared 2 take u there But understand the rulez of flight
There R no secrets 2 this ride, confide and hold me tight
Our possibilities R infinite our pleasures obvious
Heaven on earth can only be seen by a team unified in trust

2 Angela
from 2PAC (signed)

Okay enough of the land of poetry 4 now back to u.
We'll discuss the (youth) program when u come visit so I'll
save that 4 later. I'm glad I am in your thoughts on a regular basis that means a lot 2 me and really it's very much
appreciated and mutual! I C it's time 4 u & I to move up a
notch huh ☺! Okay here we go we have just moved into
level 2 of this unorthodox relationship! Okay enough rest!
You ready 4 fantasy land? Well what'z the matter cat got
ya tongue ☺ follow me to fantasy

FANTASY #1

Ms. Angela worked hard 2 day. Another day of overaggressive business suits and hormone crazy bosses but finally work was over and she headed home. She was having daily daydreams about her penitentiary bound pen-pal but he had at least 6 months 2 do B4 she could finally C him. So she thought about her replacements. Usually Reggie was always good 4 a fuck but lately he'd been letting his imagination of a wife & his fragile feelings get involved and that was a no-no! Reggie didn't have the heart 2 possess what she owned naturally. There was always Tim but he was a rotten lover his only saving grace was his insatiable fettish 4 eating pussy but tonight she needed more than just a tongue 2 appease the burning desire that flamed from her stomach down 2 her pink parts! She needed a complete passionate equally insatiable MAN and lately they were scarce in these parts. As she pulled up in her drive way she tried to decide between Tim & Reggie, maybe she could have them both shit who was she kidding between the both of them she couldn't "come" if she paid 4 it. She put her key in the door but it was open. She pushed the door open and cautiously walked inside. She flipped the light switch but no light appeared. She moved slowly 2 the living room 2 find a candle burning leaving the room immersed in a glow of mystery. There was a note beneath the candle:

UNDRESS AND GO TO
TUB RIGHT NOW DON'T SAY
A WORD OR WHISPER OR FACE
EXTREME PUNISHMENT U HAVE
3 MINUTES 2 BE NAKED AND WET!

Quickly she made a sweeping inventory of all the lovers of her past but she could not remember one so forceful and . . . . sexy! She quickly undressed and walked gracefully toward the bathroom. Her breast held firmly bouncing slightly as she entered the bathroom several candles were burning around the steaming bubble bath she slipped inside the water and for the first time noticed a walkman laying beside the tub with another note!:

U WERE 30 SECONDS
LATE I WILL DEAL WITH
THAT LATER.
PRESS PLAY!

She pressed play and a voice instantly had her enraptured and captive. The man on the tape spoke forcefully but assuringly enticing. He spoke deeply but almost at a whisper barely audible beneath the sounds of the bubble bath. She turned up the volume his voice was deliberate and inviting as he spoke these words.

"Angela lay back and relax let the warmth of the water bring back forgotten moments in the womb. Close your eyes and use your other senses feel the water protecting U from the cold miserable world smell the incense I have burning throughout the house listen 2 the waves of the water as it soothes you. Listen! Take your hands and place them in your hair and wet them until it hangs off of your head wipe your face of all the phoney smiles u unleashed today wipe your chest of all the stress u have stored there rub your stomach and feel the hunger for passion u possess. Now place your hands over your "life giver" and caress yourself 4 a moment. Place a finger over your clitoris and gently rub. Place a another finger inside of you. Gently stroke & rub simultaneously until u feel a warm sensation in your stomach then stop and stand up"

As Angela followed every step in the letter she felt the stirring hunger bursting from her stomach. She began 2 stand when she could smell the presence of a man. It was unmistakable. She then felt two soft gentle but firm hands guide her to the kitchen a cloth table covering was placed on the table and she was layed out on the table on her back with her eyes still held tightly shut. She could hear the fridge door opening. Then she felt the presence over her. She felt the warm rush of his wet mouth as he kissed her lips then her chin then her neck up 2 her ears behind her neck down her arms up her elbow 2 her belly button up her stomach across her breast around her hard nipples up 2 her neck over each earlobe then back down her stomach WOW! She clinched and gripped the table as the ice cube slid across her stomach. Using his mouth the "presence" licked her breast from inch to inch concentrating on the nipples. After melting the first two she quivered as he opened her legs and placed his frigid but soft tongue into her licking and flicking until she grabbed his head and moaned in exstacy. He built up his technique into a frenzied rush and had her twitching from his touch. He pour warm honey over her and licked as he squeezed a lemon til it dripped on her private parts. He placed his honey drenched finger into her vagina. She moaned at the depth of his penetration. He pulled his finger from the warmth of her essence and ordered her 2 open her mouth. She licked the man's finger and enjoyed the lemonade tasting AMBROSIA. He parted her legs further and put the head of his person into her pink parts. She clinched up and released a gasp as he slowly inserted

half of his staff into her she arched her back 2 meet the
dominance of his entrance but he pulled it out mid stroke
and massaged & rubbed the surrounding area of her vagina
again he repeated his initial entrance until her moans became unbearable then he entered her fully in one merciless stroke. She clutched him in her arms like the owner
of the last breath. She kissed him blindly 2 keep from
yelling in passion he rhythmically stroked her in various
speeds and intensities 4 at least 30 minutes before he
picked her up & carried her into the living room he placed
her on the carpet and placed her on her stomach he then
put a couch pillow under her belly as he entered her from
behind. He rode her with a slow controlled pace then
abruptly switching 2 a wild vigorous frenzy intermittently.
He lifted her once again and lay himself on the bed and
she straddled him and felt his manhood pierce her inside
like a spear. She swore she could feel him entering her
throat then he got up and grabbed several articles of clothing and tied her up 2 the 4 corners of the massive bed then
he spoke "OPEN YOUR EYES NOW" By the time Angela
opened her eyes her pen pal was already inside her stroking
her like an Olympic longshoremen. LONG SATISFYING
COMPLETE STROKES. As she formed her mouth 2 say
his name he picked her up and they were standing with her
back 2 the wall with her legs in his arm as he impaled
her until she screamed his name in orgasmic intensity.
OH GOD 2PAC!!

See Ya in
Fantasy #2 Boo!

NEXT STOP

Okay that's all 4 this trip. I got another favor and I hope u do this 4 me it's slightly crazy! Okay here's my favor. At midnite each nite until u see me touch yourself and whisper my name 20 times. PLEASE ANGELA? Would U Do that 4 me? I don't care whose next 2 u BLOCK them out and let me have some every night Just give me 20 strokes and calls and I'll do the same. In time it will be real and those will be 20 of the sweetest most heartfelt intense strokes in the history of lovemaking. So please "friend" Do that 4 me. Don't go all fast I want 20 slow meaningful strokes then u can go back 2 the dud next 2 u. He can't compare 2 this shit we got. C ya tonight at midnite Lover!

PASSIONATELY
2PAC (SIGNED)

Pac,

I am taken by your confidence; your knowingness of a woman's mind, body, and yearnings; your ability to seduce with letters that form your words that develop into sentences that create your lovely paragraphs and stories and poetry. (What a mouthful!!!! ☺) My roommate and I think you should teach a class to all the men of the world and let them know that it's okay to be sensitive, emotional, romantic, and passionate. It's okay! Tell the men in the prison that it's okay!!! Scream it from your cell. *It's okay!!!!* ☺ I'm trippin', right? ☺

I wanted to let you know that I appreciate your straightforwardness. I used to question whether or not your being in prison was the reason for your honesty and directness, but I feel that questioning your personality because of where you are is not fair to our thang. I am trusting that your words are real and that your emotions are yours, regardless of the confinement. I have emotions for you, too, and I've never met you either. I think about you constantly, dream of you, daydream about us, wish, fantasize, and wonder about a lot of things pertaining to you and me. Hell, at the beginning of this unorthodox relationship, I had us married before I'd even received your first letter. ☺ Funny, right? Yeah, I know. It's a female thing. But hey, everyone fantasizes. It's only human.

I'm sending you a poem that will answer your request about midnight. Not a problem. Keep your head up, Pac. Everything is going to work out. Just know that there is a plan for you, and patience is needed on your part to see it through. I got your back, Boo! ☺

"Keep ya head up!" ☺.

Forever,
Angela

My Promise to You

(Written exclusively for Tupac Shakur by Angela Ardis)

Once upon a time I made a promise to you
At midnight there was something you asked me to do
To myself, with you in mind, I see stars shining bright
Then my eyes I do close in the darkness of night . . .

My breathing is calm as your face appears above me
My body is positioned just how you want it to be
You lower your body and kiss me gently on the lips
You take a soft pillow and elevate my hips . . .

I can feel your hands as they find a path up my thighs
In the darkness of night I let out several sighs
Of passion and lust as your fingers rest on my mound
And from a distance I can hear a humming sound . . .

My vibrator as your tongue or your fingers or both
It goes down past my mound with 20 slow strokes
One . . . my head turns with the slowest of ease
Two . . . my muscles begin to slowly squeeze

Three . . . my mouth parts as his name slips out
Four . . . I begin to sensually squirm about
Five . . . my breathing is louder and a small grin appears
Six . . . I can see him above me I can see him quite clear

Seven . . . my other hand rests on my chest
Eight . . . my vibrator is doing what it does best
Nine . . . my body moves with a rhythmic beat
Ten . . . I'm feeling chills from my head to me feet

Eleven . . . my nipples are hard as I caress them in my hand
Twelve . . . my head raises up and on the pillow it will land
Thirteen . . . my hand slides down and parts my two lips
Fourteen . . . my vibrator's moving to the motion of my hips

Fifteen . . . my moans and groans are quite intense
Sixteen . . . my body locks up with suspense
Seventeen . . . my breathing is erratic as sweat begins to form
Eighteen . . . my temperature has risen it has gotten quite warm

Nineteen . . . I'm screaming, Don't stop! Don't stop!
Twenty . . . Oh God! Tupac . . . Tupac . . . Tupac . . . Tupac . . .
Tupac . . . Tupac . . . Tupac . . . Tupac . . . Tupac . . . Tupac . . . Tupac . . .
Tupac . . .
Tupac . . . Tupac . . . Tupac . . . Tupac . . . Tupac . . . Tupac . . . Tupac . . .
Tupac . . .

We were somewhere else, in a place that no one else had ever been able to take me to before, and I was enjoying every minute of it!

Chapter 14

ANTICIPATION

Tupac Shakur #95A1140
CLINTON CORRECTIONAL FACILITY

P O BOX 2001

DANNEMORA N Y 12929
 E-5-16

Ms. Angela "Lovely" Ardis
1404 Summit Springs Drive
 Dunwoody, GA. 30350

Dearest Angela, 👁, Just recieved your letter! Thanx Boo 4
being so understanding that makes this relationship that much
more special 2 me. Every word u wrote was felt deeply. Thanx Baby!
That showed just how much of a woman u R! Now did I
tell u how much i enjoyed the pictures? I didn't huh.
Well check it I LOVED THE PICTUREZ
all of 'em the sexiest shots were the baby pictures oh child
u had it going on from birth make a nigga wanna meet ya
daddy! 🙂 Basically as long as we keep the honesty between us
U and I will be fine, even better than fine! I'm looking
Forward 2 seeing u soon! I hope by now u recieved my
letter (package) I'll be sending a follow-up real soon. This
letter was specifically 4 u 2 know how much I
appreciated your response 2 my letter. How impressed
I was by your unconditional friendship. Like I said.
Get through this and can't nothing fuck with our
thang! MS. Lovely!

ONE LOVE
BOO!

2 NIGHT

Tonight 👀, search the skiez
In Hopes 2 find a star
A promise made from far away
2 Locate where U R
A Comfort-zone when you're alone
No other man will find
They taste the fruitz of paradise
But fail 2 feed your mind
Tonight 👀 Search the skiez 2 find
My Agony won't hide
Within my deepest thoughts I cry
These tearz of lonely timez
Whatever will Become of us
I wonder 2 the Moon
Will i be blessed At last possess
The pleasure found with u
Unique & Rare so Hard 2 find
Someone 2 trust 4 Life
Foreplay is a must 4 us plus I'll fuck u Right
Don't blush from wordz of truth
Ask your self "is He 4 real"?
Free 2 Search my Soul & Heart Now tell me if u feel me

4 Angela ☺ Epic

WHEN GEMINIZ COLLIDE!

The Moon iz full the starz so bright
The heavens fill with Pride
When Thoughts Connect hearts exchanged
And Geminiz collide
The most criminal of Men surrender 2 sin
And change thier lives from liez
When they embrace thier destined fate
As Geminis collide
No longer Alone subject 2 pain
The victim in us died
At last we Kiss And then witness
When geminiz collide!

4 Angela
By 2Pac

181

Dearest Angela,

I just received your letter! Thanx Boo 4 being so understanding that makes this relationship that much more
special 2 me. Every word u wrote was felt deeply. Thanx
baby! That showed just how much of a woman U R! Now
did I tell you how much I enjoyed the pictures? I didn't
huh. Well check it I LOVED THE PICTURES! All of 'em the
sexiest shots were the baby pictures. Oh child U had it
going on from birth make a nigga wanna meet ya daddy!
☺ Basically as long as we keep the honesty between us U
and I we'll be fine, even better than fine! I'm looking forward 2 seeing U soon! I hope by now U received my letter
(package) I'll be sending a follow-up real soon. This letter
was specifically 4 U 2 know how much I appreciated your
response 2 my letter. How impressed I was by your unconditional friendship. Like I said get through this and
can't nothing fuck with our <u>thang</u>! Ms. Lovely!

ONE LOVE
BOO!
2PAC (Signed)

2 NIGHT

Tonight I search the skiez
In hopes 2 find a star
A promise made from far away
2 locate where U R
A comfort zone when you're alone
No other man will find
They taste the fruitz of paradise
But fail 2 feed your mind
Tonight I search the skiez to find
My agony won't hide
Within my deepest thoughts I cry
These tearz of lonely timez
Whatever will become of us
I wonder to the moon
Will I be blessed at last possess
The pleasure found with U
Unique & rare so hard 2 find
Someone 2 trust 4 life
Foreplay is a must 4 us plus I'll fuck U right
Don't blush from wordz of truth
Ask yourself "Is he 4 real"?
Free 2 search my soul & heart now tell me if U feel me

☺

4 Angela! *2PAC*

WHEN GEMINIZ COLLIDE!

The moon iz full the starz so bright
The heavens fill with pride
When thoughts connect hearts exchanged
And geminiz collide
The most criminal of men surrender 2 sin
And change their lives from liez
When they embrace their destined fate
As geminis collide
No longer alone subject 2 pain
The victim in us died
At last we kiss and then witness
When geminiz collide!

4 Angela
By 2PAC (Signed)

Tupac,

I loved your poems. You know I did. ☺ I'm a little under the weather today, and I left work because of it. I was feeling a little nauseated and faint, and I couldn't figure out for the life of me what the problem was. I thought maybe I had had too much coffee this morning. Well, after throwing every-thing around and coming up with absolutely nothing, I told my boss that I had to go home and I left.

Weeeeeeeellllllll, as I drove home, I started to get more sick, but I didn't have to throw up. Then I began thinking and realized that I hadn't taken a dump in at least four days. ☺ Imagine that. I'm sick because I'm full of shit. So I came home and put a Ducolax in my body, and now I'm waiting for it to take effect. That's a lot of information, isn't it? (Haaaaaaaaaa!)

You know, I've been thinking about our letters, and I just don't want you to get out of there and, if we decide to take it to an intimate level, come and run through me. That wouldn't make me smile, but I guess that's something that we have control over. I guess. Oh . . . oh . . . uh oh . . . hold on . . .

I'm back. Wheeeeewwwwww! I feel much better now. My laxative finally kicked in, and man, what a relief that was. I'm glad you're not here to smell the madness that erupted in my bathroom!! (Haaaaaaaaaaaaaaa!) That's nasty, isn't it? I know, I can't help myself sometimes. But I'll have you know that I did take a shower and washed my body, so I'm not sit-ting here writing you with a stinky tooshy. (Haaaaaaaaaaa!) I crack myself up. Okay now, where were we ☺?

Oh, my mother likes the song "Dear Mama." Of course she would, right? She's coming around with this whole me-coming-to-visit-you thing. She'll be fine. Everything will be fine.

I can't wait to meet you and take this off paper. You feel me?

I found this stuff on love between Geminis:

This relationship will put you in paradise or be a total disaster. You'll get that strange feeling on being introduced for the first time that you've met before. Miss Gemini will certainly reflect a lot of what is going on in your head. When you two are together, you'll never be at a loss for words. You both like to flit about and hate the idea of being hemmed in. So long as you enjoy wandering together, all will be well. Romance with this woman born under the same sign as you is likely to be passionate. You should have a pretty good idea of her sexual needs and desires. You are both imaginative so your bedroom scenes will never become a bore. She'll appreciate your aims and desires because she feels the same urges. Gemini men very often form platonic friendships with Gemini women. You have no difficulty getting along as long as there's no emotional element.

I have already told you that I feel like I've known you for years. It's crazy, but hey! Such is life. Stay strong, Pac. This too shall pass.

Forever,
Angela

Extreme Dream

(Written exclusively for Tupac from Angela)

I woke up one day and had a realization that I couldn't believe
It didn't seem possible, all-be-it real, it was hard to conceive

I flipped it around in my head knowing it couldn't be what it seemed
So I chalked it up, tossed it out, and labeled it an Extreme Dream

But then the voice was heard, then the letter, and soon I'll see
The man in my dreams will be standing before me
I can't blink my eyes, pinch my arm, or slap myself to wake up
Fruition, culmination, fulfillment, final result won't be abrupt

You're invading my dreams, suspended throughout my day
You've taking over my hands as letters float your way
You've got my mind wrapped in nothing but thoughts of you
Anticipations, expectations, probabilities about what to do

But until we meet standing still in time
I will continue to inhale you erasing any lines
Inhibitions, reticence, the shyness that won't be seen
I'll lay back finding comfort in my Extreme Dreams

The night air was full and warm. The flickering of the candle was even and steady, letting off an aroma that filled our screened-in porch. Tan and I had decided that tonight was our "girl time." Wine coolers chilled in the ice chest, empty Chinese food boxes covered the table that separated our lounge chairs, and Mary J. Blige crooned "You Gotta Believe" through the night air.

"What do you think it's going to be like when you're finally face to face?" Tan asked.

I opened my eyes and found a star gazing down at me. "I don't know."

"That's the star I sent you every night," Tupac said, pointing into the sky.
"How do you know it was that star, Pac?" I asked.
"Look at it," he said, pointing. "It's the biggest and the

brightest." He smiled, taking another sip of his
champagne.

I lay on the blanket with my hands behind my head and
just gazed at his silhouette, cast by the moon. He lay
beside me, resting on one arm, holding his glass of champagne in the other hand. I stared at him while he watched
the rise and fall of my midriff with each breath I took. He
poured champagne on my stomach, and my stomach muscles contracted as I laughed. He descended, kissing and
licking everywhere the champagne fell. We were out in the
open. We were being spied on by the very stars we had
wished on, said good night to, and hoped our mutual feelings were being transferred through. It was soothing. It felt
like the entire world had stopped just to allow us to lay
there, suspended in time, enjoying what we had fantasized
for so many nights.

He made his way north to my neck, his hands covering
the uncharted territory that he seemed so familiar with. He
looked down at me and smiled.

"Ms. Lovely," he said softly. "You want some more to
drink?" he asked, raising the glass to his mouth, coming
close to mine, then taking a swallow of the champagne. I
reached for the glass. He pulled it away, shaking his head
no.

"I'll give it to you, but you have to tell me that you want
it. You want some more to drink?" he asked playfully, de-
scending toward my lips.

"You want some more to drink?" Tan's voice was barely audible,
but it sounded like Tupac's.

"Yes . . . yes, I want some . . . yes," I said breathily, until I realized I was dreaming and—guess who ruined it *again*? Tanya slowly
handed me another cooler.

"Girl, what were you dreaming about?" Tanya said, smiling. "I wish I had been there."

I took a deep breath, found the brightest star, and smiled. It was midnight.

Chapter 15

HE TRULY NEEDED A HUG

Tupac Shakur # 95A1140
CLINTON CORRECTIONAL FACILITY

P O BOX ___Zoo1___

DANNEMORA N Y 12929

E-5-16

Ms. Angela Ardis
1404 Summit Springs Dr,
Dunwoody, GA. 30350

April 3, 1995

Dear Angela,
            I got ya letter and Ms. lovely u Are a fucking
riot. I laughed my ass off! It is rare 2 hear a
female be so honest & open. I'm glad u feel so comfortable
with me, as well u should. U have nothing 2 fear with me.
The information on the Gemini Love thang was highly insightful
Almost scary. How R U? Did u recieve my letter, & Poem.
Did u like it? I have all of your pictures up and
each night I create another fantasy 2 encompass each
one in time I hope they all become reality. No love
I won't come home & run through u. That's not my
style. I am serious about us being friends
and don't doubt my intentions on that! As
long as we keep it open & real with each other u and I
have a future. Only dishonesty & greed can destruct this.
Can u feel me? ☺ I can feel u strongly believe that!
I wrote u 3 new poems. I hope u enjoy them. Know
that u R in my heart & mind and that each day i feel u.
Keep the faith, Tell mom's thanx 4 the understanding &
support & I owe u a 5 star dinner remind me
while we're catching up on lost time 2 stop long
enough 2 show u my Culinary skills. If I'm
in your system Now wait til i cook then it's all
over you'll want 2 get a tatoo and everything ☺
                                        Eternal
                                        FRIEND 2PAC

TIME

Today we exchange promises
Tonight we pray their kept
In the Morning We Wake 2 Face Tomorrow
Anticipation on each breath

4 The Moment we accept our situation
In the hopes they change in time
Heaven is Love, Hell is lonliness
Yet they both exist in our minds

Some Say friends are overrated
Hard 2 find and Quick 2 change
And Even i believed this true
until the day u came

Yesterday I wanted Death
Because my future was plagued with Pain
But Now i've found a friend in u
Now i've learned 2 live again.

Angela
FROM
CATE

2 fuck the taste from YOUR MOUTH

A Naughty Poem by T. Shakur
Exclusively 4 Angela

Let me fuck the taste from your Mouth
give me kiss AND close your eyes
Tonight's the Night I love u Right
Lay back and enjoy the ride

Grab hold of Something stable
Forgive me if I Ignore
Your Screams and Moans oohs and aahs
and continue 2 give u more

Would u mind if slept inside u
2 awake in heaven's gate
then would it be cool if I drooled on u
then kiss & licked your face

Let me fuck the taste from your mouth
Then sleep and rest Peacefully
Now No Matter Who comes B4 or After
u got the Best piece from Me

2 Angela

Am I Naughty
or What?

Possession 4 Angela by 2Pac

In My Heart there lives a Small child
eager 2 Love anxious 2 please
Destined 2 change the Merciless souls
And infect the world like disease

In My mind there lives a great soldier
fearless in Motion relentless in stride
In search of the ones intent to destroy
This paradise built from inside

In my soul there lives an adventurer
ready 2 die quick 2 explore
hungry 4 ~~change~~ change they battle My brain
one Man possessed By All Four

Wanting 2 Free My spirit
But the world aint ready 2 C
Through stress and pain I struggle 2 gain
A place in this world 4 Me

April 3, 1995

Dear Angela,

I got ya letter and Ms. Lovely U are a fucking riot. I laughed my ass off! It is rare 2 hear a female so honest & open. I'm glad U feel so comfortable with me, as well U should. U have nothing to fear with me. The information on the Gemini love thang was highly insightful. Almost scary. How R U? Did U receive my letter & poem. Did U like it? I have all of your pictures up and each night I create another fantasy 2 encompass each one in time I hope to become reality. No love I won't come home & run through U. That's not my style. I am serious about us being friends and don't doubt my intentions on that! As long as we keep it open & real with each other U and I have a future. Only dishonesty & greed can destruct this can u feel me? ☺ I can feel U strongly believe that! I wrote U 3 new poems. I hope U enjoy them. Know that U R in my heart & mind and that each day I feel U. Keep the faith, tell mom's thanx 4 the understanding & support & I owe U a 5 star dinner remind me while we're catching up on lost time 2 stop long enough 2 show U my culinary skills. If I'm in your system now wait til I cook then it's all over you'll want 2 get a tattoo and everything. ☺

Eternal Friend
2PAC (signed)

TIME

Today we exchange promises
Tonight we pray their kept
In the morning we wake 2 face tomorrow
Anticipation on each breath

4 the moment we accept our situation
In the hopes they change in time
Heaven is love, hell is lonliness
Yet they both exist in our minds

Some say friends are overrated
Hard 2 find and quick 2 change
And even I believed this true
Until the day u came

Yesterday I wanted death
Because my future was plagued with pain
But now I've found a friend in u
Now I've learned 2 live again

2 Angela
from
2PAC (signed)

Exclusively 4 Angela

2 FUCK THE TASTE FROM YOUR MOUTH

A Naughty poem by T. Shakur

Let me fuck the taste from your mouth
Give me kiss and close your eyes
Tonight's the night I love U right
Lay back and enjoy the ride

Grab hold of something stable
Forgive me if I ignore
Your screams and moans oohs and aahs
And continue 2 give U more

Would U mind if I slept inside U
2 awake in heaven's gate
then would it be cool if I drooled on U
then kiss & licked your face

Let me fuck the taste from your mouth
Then sleep and rest peacefully
Now no matter who comes B4 or after
U got the best piece from me

2 Angela
☺
2PAC (signed)
Am I naughty
or what?

4 Angela by 2PAC
POSSESSION

In my heart there lives a small child
Eager to love anxious 2 please
Destined 2 change merciless souls
And infect the world like disease

In my mind there lives a great soldier
Fearless in motion relentless in stride
In search of the ones intent to destroy
This paradise built from inside

In my soul there lives an adventurer
Ready 2 die quick 2 explore
Hungry 4 change they battle my brain
One man possessed by all four

Wanting 2 free my spirit
But the world ain't ready 2 C
Through stress and pain I struggle 2 gain
A place in this world 4 me

Pac,

   One of your poems seemed a little down to me. Are you okay? Aside from the normal, are you okay? I wish I could come and hold you and rock you till you fell asleep. The illusion of the dark corner probably doesn't lend much comfort when the walls are closing in, huh? I wish I had something magical I could say to make everything bearable and to bring a smile to your face other than the fact that I have bowel issues from time to time ☺. Okay, okay, no more of that. What's going on in there? Is your family okay? Is Keisha okay? Is your business okay? I don't know, Boo. Talk to me. Don't shut me out.

I can feel you as much as you feel me. You're inside me now. In a special place in my heart and soul that I didn't even know existed. You are giving me feelings and emotions that I've never had and don't believe I'll ever find again. It's special, and I want to hold on to it forever, however long forever may be for us (eternity ☺). Like you said, Pac, I don't have the answers for yesterday, today, or tomorrow but I do know how I feel about you, and I know that I want this to remain a positive "friendship," full of life and realness. Can you feel me? You are such a special person, and some of the weight you carry around on your shoulders you need to release. It's not yours to carry. Not all of it. But I know, being a Gemini, we have a loyalty to those we love and care about, and we will sacrifice ourselves many times in an effort to make someone comfortable or even happy for a second. Material items mean nothing to us if we can't share them with the ones we love. I feel you, Pac, right now, during my day and definitely at midnight ☺. Keep your head up, Boo. I'll be there soon, and we'll see if I can replace your frown with a smile.

Forever,
Angela

Never Feel Lonely You're Never Alone
(Written exclusively for Pac from Angela)

The world can be cruel when the wind blows down
Left alone, nowhere to turn, people once there can't be found

Searching for the reality you thought was yours for life
All the pain, headaches and heartache were the lows of strife

But turn around PAC there are people out there
People who've been there since day one that truly care
About your well-being, dilemmas, your mental state of mind
Open your eyes, unblock your ears, in your heart please find

The realness in those around you those your instincts do dare
To challenge your impulse, to test your senses towards those who
don't care
Find the realness in your world and know that it will prevail
Those are the people who will be down when all else fails

I'm new to your life but am concerned just the same
Don't care about your money, material bullshit or fame
It's Tupac I'm writing and feeling in my heart
Realizing the connection appreciating your realness from the start

So as you sit there assessing the hand that life dealt you
Know people love you and care about the things that you do
Take heed in your next hand and avoid that to which you're prone
And know that you should never feel lonely because you're never
alone.

Special Place

(Written exclusively for PAC from Angela)

Is there something I can say to bring a smile to your face
Is there somewhere we can go A special hiding place
Where everything you enjoy is abundant and free

If I figure it out would you come with me

We could run around enlightened by the openness of space
We could lay in silence as the sun washes our face
We could talk by the river as the water cools our feet
In this place I could find it would be simple and sweet

We could eat all the foods without a care in the world
We could light a fire and inside the blanket stay curled
We could erase all that ails and weighs heavily on our minds
I'll find a place PAC and everything will be fine

To escape the world's bulk for seconds, minutes, or days
To revive all that's dead inside and attempt to find new ways
To see the beauty life has to offer from everything around
I've got a secret to tell you this place has been found

I can't tell you in this poem because someone might see
This secret is between us just for you and for me
So anticipate the answer as I continue to lure
And I'll tell you tonight in our dark corner

A man of Tupac's stature couldn't find a place in this world for himself? A place to rest, a place for his inner child to run worry-free and be nurtured by those who truly care? I just felt sorry for him. He truly needed a hug.

I wanted to comfort him, to reach out and embrace him or lift his burdens, but I couldn't. I could do only what I was doing, which was write letters and poetry and hope that they helped him cope in some way. Hope that they reached that place within him that needed to be uplifted.

Hope that they made a difference somehow.

I SEND AN INVITATION

Tupac Shakur # 95A1140
CLINTON CORRECTIONAL FACILITY

P O BOX 2001

DANNEMORA N Y 12929
E-5-16

Ms. Angela Ardis
1404 Summit Springs DR.
Dunwoody, GA. 30350

Sorry it took so long i ran
out of stamps and had
to wait for
store day.

April 6, 1995

Dearest Angela;

what u felt in my last letter was just my slight depression,
don't worry about it though it passes, sometimes i get that way. It's just
so hard to have to go through all of this when i'm innocent. the feeling
of helplessness brings anger, sadness and then depression but i'm working
on that. Today i got a visit from Jada & M.C. Lyte it was cool, very funny
but somewhat distant. Yo-Yo wants me to write a song 4 her. Lyte
wants me to write a song for her album & Digital underground wants
the same thing so I'm trying 2 stay busy. I'm back to working on
these scripts I've been writing. I have four; A MAN'z World,
KINDRED SPIRIT2, MERCY STREET and MY BROTHER'S KEEPER.
hopefully it will be my ticket to reclaiming what's rightfully mine. the world.
☺ So if I seem distant or depressed try 2 understand sweetheart it isn't
personal it's just the situation calls 4 it. what's up with u ms. lovely?
u shit yet ☺! Haa Haa) Right now it's late I don't know what time it is
but it's mid-morning everyone is asleep and i just popped up from my sleep
feeling u 4 the moment. I just looked at all your pictures. I told
Kesha about your comments concerning me not being realistic she
was surprised at your realness but it helped to reinforce how cool
I told her u was. I hope u don't mind. I thought about what u
said it made sense but let me elaborate. Call me an alien, but i truly
believe u can love more than one person it may not be an identical love
but it can be just as genuine. 9 example u can have more than one person
so why not vice versa. U fear more than one thing so why not vice versa.
I don't feel any guilt or sense of deception when i write u or "flirt"
as u put it because it is my nature and it is sincere. I may not
know how it will all turn out but i have faith that it will fall into place
when the time is right. All i can do is open my heart and be honest
and hope 4 understanding. Is that being greedy? selfish? I
don't have all the answers I just know I want happiness and
I am happy when i am true 2 my heart and at this point that
has been the case. I'm curious 2 c how we progress over time

203

I can't lie I am totally at a loss 4 what the future holds but i have this fear you'll change heart or lose interest. It's not my wish but as with life it will be out of my hands, that's why i don't hold back with U 2 be sure I tell u & share all that i am offering U. That way I know u feel me and as long as u do Nothing & Nobody can replace me. I know it may be a confusing situation but I ask that u challenge your sense of reality and follow our path til it ends (if it ends☺) and see what becomes of this "intense pen pal thing". Is that fair? If im correct you should be coming 2 c me soon huh? I'm definitely looking forward to it. I keep visualizing the moment we stand face 2 face what will happen? will i kiss U? Will i be nervous? Will i feel u once u R B4 me? it's definitely intense! What R U thinking? Tell me. R U Nervous? Excited? What, tell me something. Angela!☺ U Bored with me yet? Be honest! 4 us 2 survive the changing currents we have to be eternally honest and communicate okay? Now that i'm in your system i don't want 2 leave ☺! Well get back 2 me Share your heart with me. Keep ya Head up. Keep the faith. Remember Midnight. Keep my presence in your heart and C U Soon. I can't wait 2 C what u wear, I know it's going 2 be a headbanger! I Remain —

Eternally

P.S. Thanks 4 Easing the pain in my Heart tonight! I owe U one!

April 6, 1995

Dearest Angela,

   What U felt in my last letter was just my slight depression, don't worry about it though it passes. Sometimes I get that way. It's just so hard to have to go through all of this when I'm innocent. The feeling of helplessness brings anger, sadness and then depression but I'm working on that. Today I got a visit from Jada & M.C. Lyte it was cool, very funny but somewhat distant. Yo-Yo wants me to write a song 4 her. Lyte wants me to write a song for her album & Digital Underground wants the same thing so I'm trying 2 stay busy. I'm back to working on these scripts I've been writing. I have four, A MAN'Z WORLD, KINDRED SPIRITZ, MERCY STREET and MY BROTHER'S KEEPER. Hopefully it will be my ticket to reclaiming what's rightfully mine . . . The World. ☺ So if I seem distant or depressed try 2 understand sweetheart it isn't personal It's just the situation calls for it. What's up with U Ms. Lovely? U shit yet? (☺ ! Haa Haa) Right now it's late I don't know what time it is but it's mid-morning everyone is asleep and I just popped up from my sleep feeling U 4 the moment. I just looked at all your pictures. I told Keisha about your comments concerning me not being realistic she was surprised by your realness but it helped to reinforce how cool I told her U was. I hope U don't mind. I thought about what U said it made sense but let me elaborate. Call me an alien, but I truly believe U can love more than one person it may not be an identical love but it can be just as genuine. 4 example U can hate more than one person so why not vice versa. U fear more than one thing so why not vice versa. I don't feel any guilt or sense of deception when

I write U or "flirt" as u put it because it is my nature and it is sincere. I may not know how it will all turn out but I have faith that it will fall into place when the time is right. All I can do is open my heart and be honest and hope 4 understanding. Is that being greedy? Selfish? I don't have all the answers I just know I want happiness and I am happy when I am true 2 my heart and at this point that has been the case. I'm curious 2 C how we progress over time. I can't lie I am totally at a loss 4 what the future holds but I have this fear you'll change heart or lose interest. It's not my wish but as with life it will be out of my hands. That's why I don't hold back with U 2 be sure I tell U & share all that I am offering U. That way I know u feel me and as long as U do, nothing & nobody can replace me. I know it may be a confusing situation but I ask that u challenge your sense of reality and follow our path til it ends (if it ends ☺) and see what becomes of this "intense pen pal thing." Is that fair? If I'm correct you should be coming 2 C me soon huh? I'm definitely looking forward to it. I keep visualizing the moment we stand face 2 face what will happen? Will I kiss U? Will I be nervous? Will I feel U once U R B4 me? It's definitely intense! What R U thinking? Tell me. R U nervous? Excited? What, tell me something Angela! ☺ U bored with me yet? Be honest! 4 us 2 survive the changing currents we have to be eternally honest and communicate okay? Now that I'm in your system I don't want 2 leave ☺! Well get back 2 me. Share your heart with me. Keep ya head up. Keep the faith. Remember midnight. Keep my presence in your heart and C U soon. I can't wait 2 C what U wear, I know it's going 2 be a <u>headbanger</u>! I remain—

ETERNALLY
2PAC (signed)

P.S. Thanks 4 easing the pain in
My heart tonight I owe U one!

2PAC (signed)

Dear Pac,

Hey, what's up with you? I just read the article you did in *Vibe*. I'm glad to hear that you're done with all that "Thuglife" stuff. I see you've been thinking in there. ☺ I guess once you put the herb down, it allowed your mind to see the things that weren't so evident before. I hope your people and Queen are assisting you by holding their own, along with the help that you give. I know that people tend to get lazy and live off the help, and get amnesia when it comes to taking care of themselves when someone such as yourself is so giving.

I'm glad that work is keeping you busy. The scriptwriting is good, Pac. You're a hot commodity, and you're a natural when it comes to your abilities. I think the industry will readily embrace all that you have to offer. Just keep it coming ☺.

I don't mind you talking to Keisha about what I wrote. It's not a surprise to me. It's cool, and I would expect you to. She is your Queen, right? No secrets.

I also want you to know that I do not consider you an alien. I understand and agree with your views on loving more than one person, but at the same time, you have to make distinct differentiations among those loves when trying to narrow down your life partner. If you even believe in life partners and marriage. Don't misunderstand where I'm coming from. I just feel that when you love someone on the level you love Keisha (the Queen status level ☺), that love should be stronger and more powerful than the others to the point that straying away from her isn't an option. Temptation is a bitch, PAC, but you should know better than most that no matter what temptation is offering your manhood, or how fine she is, or how fine her clothes are, or how tight her body is, or how electric the chemistry becomes, once you've hit it, the thrill of the chase or conquest is gone. Not to mention that you have an aftermath to deal with, and that's Keisha, if she's the Queen of your life. Whether you tell her or not, your mind will get the best of you, and whether she lets you know that she's aware of your conquests, she'll also be eaten away by her mind every time you're not home, don't call right back, or just simply go to work. It's a man thing at times, but it's also disrespectful and devalues you as a man to your woman. In that I mean that our man, initially, is a prize to most women. The one who loves them, comes home to them, cherishes them. How lucky we feel to have found a "good one." But you become less and less of a "good one" with each lie and conquest. Put it this way: winning a first-place prize doesn't make you feel special if you have to share it with other competitors. My opinion, totally my opinion. But you said you feel no guilt or deception because it's your nature and it's sincere. I'm glad to hear that. I just hope Keisha understands you as well as you think she does.☺ But like I said before, your love quotient is your own, and you two must have some kind of understanding. I'll say it again: I don't think I could be so understanding. I don't care who you are. ☺

I don't want you to fear any aspect of what we have, PAC. I can't imagine changing heart or losing interest in you. Like you said, the only things that can destroy this are lies, dishonesty, and greed. But I can't fathom you doing any of those things, nor will I. So just scratch that thought out of your head. It doesn't belong there. All of your questions are the same questions I've been asking myself. I know I'll be nervous. No doubt about it. ☺ I do have anxieties that you won't feel me once I get there, or maybe in person I won't come across like what you see in the pictures. Even though we've had phone conversations, they were all pretty short. Now we'll have actual time to talk, and what will we say? Anything? Or silence? ☺ Definitely nervous. Yup! Definitely.

I don't ever want you to leave my system, and honestly, I don't think you can. You have implanted yourself inside of me, a feeling that can be touched only by someone like you. With your frame of mind, your awareness of self, your comfort with expression, and your fearlessness of showing openness. There aren't many out there like you. None that I can name. You're one of a kind, and for that reason, you are untouchable in my emotional and psychological valleys. My system is filled with your aura, your presence, and your heart. Sappy, huh? (haaaaaa) 'Til death and beyond, PAC, you will remain. Believe that!

Forever
Angela

P.S. Midnight, Boo! Nine more hours to go. See you there! ☺

P.S.S. Hey, man, what happened to my poems? You holding back? What's up with that? ☺ Am I wrong for expecting one in every letter? You think you can come to Detroit when you get out?

Anticipation

(Written exclusively for 2Pac from Angela)

Anticipation's got my head swimming
Wonderment of what's to come
Feeling butterflies thoughts mesmerized
Of the buildup of what we've done

"Extreme Dreams" forming reality
"Stolen Kisses" reclaimed and found
"Whispers" will be spoken words
"Anticipated Ec$tacy" breeds muted sound

"Anticipation" of me standing before you
Everything culminating in the moment at hand
Will you "Feel Me"? Will emotions "Dissolve"?
These are the questions that I can't comprehend

"I Feel You" is what I keep hearing you say
Your "Possession" has taken hold
"2 Night" our visions are no longer miraged
"Time" transporting fate can be that bold?

Anticipation of our first words
The smiles that'll surely send vibrations
"I Wait" anxiously for soon when "Geminiz Collide"
That will end all "Anticipation"

INVITATION

I cordially invite you to a weekend at a cabin in the woods, where you'll find limited outside influence, peace of mind, and friendly affections that will be both therapeutic as well as mind-freeing.
In addition, there will be a star-watching vigil that is mandatory or else. ☺
DATE: Upon your release
LOCATION: Surprise and secluded
R.S.V.P.: A.S.A.P. but I know
you're cool! ☺

Chapter 17

ANOTHER SHOCKING DISCOVERY

Tupac Shakur #95A1140
CLINTON CORRECTIONAL FACILITY

P O BOX 2001

DANNEMORA N Y 12929
E-5-16

Ms. Angela Halls
1404 Summit Springs Dr.
Dunwoody, GA. 39350

My Dearest Angela,

       forgive me 4 not responding sooner it was not due to my insensitive methods of communication, rather I have been overwhelmed with drama over here. I had a physical run in with three guards and family trauma at home so I have been applying my concentration 2 these areas. thank u 4 being patient. Now let me get back 2 implanting my essence into u First of all i appreciate your concern in regards to my family friends and Queen but rest assure I am currently aware and in control on all three. There is in fact minor waves coming from my homebase "Thugmansion" but it will all turn out 4 the best. My friends in majority have been terminated and avoided, and last but not least I am enjoying a wonderful bliss with my Queen Keisha. In fact we are to be married on the 29th of April but please as a friend please keep this information a secret. Also forgive the formality of my plea it is just ~~so~~ necessary 4 me to stress the importance of my trust in you. So already I have answered two questions Is Keisha my Queen? and Do i believe in Marriage? However understand I believe in personal committment not marriage this ceremony is basically just a formality to appease the State

So that Keisha and i can recieve overnight visits. In my eyes we were already married now it is just legal. My Queen and i share our every thought and though we disagree on several issues we still ultimately support & respect each other's decisions, that is the beauty of it. Now what else did u ask me? I can't remember anyway I forgot to thank u 4 your certificate of friendship, your poem and your invitation. I would love 2 watch the stars with u. As for the trip to Detroit that would not be impossible difficult yes impossible no. The trip to the cabin in the woods very possible even welcomed. You also mentioned the decline of substance in my most recent letters. I was not aware of it but it may be because your arrival is so imminent and that excites me to the point of parolisis.. excuse my errors and shortcomings understand this prison cell does not assist in the development of the heart & mind. I sometimes succumb to the atmosphere and dive into my own consiousness. Can U feel me still? I also prohibit my writing bullshit or overdramatic promises I can never fulfill so I only write what I feel whether it be 1 page or twenty, that doesn't mean I feel less it just means I refuse to game you so

I only Included that with which I could
make a reality. If i left anything out we can discuss it
at another time. Okay Ms. lovely let's get 2 u. How do
u feel about my written intrusion to your mind.
What are your expectations. How do u truly feel
about me? Honestly Now. Where Do u see our
bond in 5 years? Enough Questions 4 U?
Okay okay No more. I'm trying to stop my
Poems to u Momentarily so that u don't
become bored or Immune to my words. feel me
Not long Just long enough to Miss. Remember
absence makes the heart grow fonder. Plus Desire
is essential to longevity and if that is indeed
what we quest then it is my duty to apply whatever
actions Necessary to keep you wanting More. Shit
Withdrawal Never hurt Nobody☺. So don't
fall off on Me. Show Some loyalty to your
willpower and we will see if u are still down 4 Me
or Not. Nah I'll probably cheat and Sneak letters 2 u
so forget that 4 Now but remember that in the future
Remember Midnite 20 strokes til death and
Keep Me In your heart at all times I Remain

Eternally
Epic

My Dearest Angela,

Forgive me 4 not responding sooner it was not due to my insensitive methods of communication, rather I have been overwhelmed with drama over here. I had a physical run in with three guards and family trauma at home so I have been applying my concentration 2 these areas. Thank U 4 being patient. Now let me get back 2 implanting my essence into U. First of all I appreciate your concern in regards to my family, friends and Queen but rest assure I am currently aware and in control on all three. There is in fact minor waves coming from my homebase "Thugmansion" but it will all turn out 4 the best. My friends in majority have been terminated and avoided and last but not least I am enjoying a wonderful bliss with my Queen Keisha. In fact we are to be married on the 29th of April but please as a friend please keep this information a secret. Also forgive the formality of my plea it is just necessary 4 me to stress the importance of my trust in you. So already I have answered two questions Is Keisha my Queen? And Do I believe in Marriage? However understand I do believe in personal commitment not marriage this ceremony is basically just a formality to appease the State so that Keisha and I can receive overnight visits. In my eyes we were already married now it is just legal. My Queen and I share our every thought and though we disagree on several issues we still ultimately support & respect each other's decisions, that is the beauty of it. Now what else did U ask me? I can't remember anyway I forgot to thank U 4 your certificate of friendship, your poem, and your invitation. I would love 2 watch the stars with U. As for the trip to Detroit that would not be impossible difficult yes impossible no. The trip to the cabin in the woods very possible even welcomed. You also mentioned the decline of substance in my most recent letters. I was not aware of it but it may be because your arrival is so imminent and that excites me to the point of paralisis excuse my errors and shortcomings understand this prison cell does not assist in the development of the heart & mind. I sometimes succumb to the atmosphere and dive into my own consiousness. Can u feel me still? I also prohibit my writing bullshit or overdramatic promises I can never fulfill so I only write what I feel whether it be 1 page or twenty. That doesn't mean I feel less it just means I refuse to game you so I only included that with which I could make a reality. If I left anything out we can discuss it at another time. Okay Ms. Lovely let's get 2 U. How do U feel about my written intrusion to your mind? What are your expectations? How do U truly feel about me? Honestly now. Where do U see our bond in 5 years? Enough questions 4 U? Okay okay no more. I'm trying to stop my poems to U momentarily so that U don't become bored or immune to my words. Feel me not long just long enough to miss. Remember absence makes the heart grow fonder. Plus desire is essential to longevity and if that is indeed what we quest then it is my duty to apply whatever actions necessary to keep you wanting more. Shit withdrawal never hurt nobody ☺. So don't fall off on me. Show some loyalty to your willpower and we will see if U are still down 4 me or not. Nah I'll probably cheat and sneak letters 2 U so forget that 4 now but remember that in the future Remember Midnite 20 strokes til death and Keep me in your heart at all times. I Remain.

ETERNALLY
2PAC (Signed)

"Married? Married?" Tanya ranted.

"Yup, married. I get it . . . I mean, he wants overnight visits. It's a means to an end," I said, tossing the idea away.

"This doesn't bother you?" she asked, watchful of my reaction.

"Yeah, it bothered me at first. But there is a method to his madness. He's doing what he has to do, to appease the state, to get what he wants," I said nonchalantly. "I can relate to that. Can't you?" I said, popping in his *Me Against the World* CD and sitting on the couch.

"No . . . I'm sure she's not aware of his intentions."

"They have a special relationship. She's his Queen," I said sarcastically. "They share the same thoughts and have no secrets. Besides, they are two adults, so who cares what the reasons are?"

She gave me a look that implied I was being irrational. Tupac's relationship with Keisha was the last thing on my mind. Besides, his minimum time of release was at least a year and a half away anyway. A lot could happen between now and then. *"So why speculate now?"* I thought.

"You're right. Two adults," Tanya said. "So he's gonna go to the cabin with you while he's married to her?"

"Well, if the marriage is one of temporary gratification, then maybe they won't stay married once he's released. He's the one who said he's interested in personal commitment and not marriage!" I was getting irritated. "I guess I'm in a catch twenty-two because my intentions for him are the same as his for me at this point. I'm not trying to disregard Keisha, but right or wrong, the way I'm feeling, if he were in front of me right now . . ."

"You'd jump him," she finished. We looked at each other knowingly.

Whether my initial intentions had been wishes, which had turned into surprised friendship, which had turned into lust, I knew that not so deep in my heart, I wanted nothing more than to explore everything that we had ever written to one another on the pages of our letters and poetry. *And more.*

"Yeah . . . well, that's a long time away, and that will be dealt with when the time comes," I said.

"You want anything from the store?" she asked.

"Yeah, a conscience." I smirked. "Naw, I'm cool. Thanks."

> *"I can't believe you're going to marry her, Pac" I said, watching the crests fall as the waves hit the shore.*
>
> *"Let's not talk about it again. We've already been there, Angela," Tupac said, holding me.*
>
> *"What are we doing? What is this?"*
>
> *"We are enjoying each other and taking advantage of every minute we get to share together. Baby, life is too short to worry about things that have no relevance to our thang," he said matter-of-factly, staring into my eyes with that everything's-okay look.*
>
> *"We don't have anything if you're spread out so thin between people that you begin to form the thin line that divides the reality between us."*
>
> *"Angela, the reality between us is here now, today, at this moment. Who knows what tomorrow will bring, if it'll come at all. Enjoy now. If tomorrow comes, we'll worry about it then. It's the moment, and now is ours," he said, pulling my face to his. He brushed his nose along my neckline and inhaled slightly.*
>
> *"You are so full of poetic shit," I mumbled.*
>
> *"I love the way you smell," he crooned. I closed my eyes as his masculinity held me hostage. "What are you thinking, Ms. Lovely?" he whispered in my ear.*
>
> *My hands made their way up his back as we looked into each other's eyes and smiled.*

"What are you thinking about?" Tanya asked, coming in the door and passing me on the couch.

"I don't believe this keeps happening," I said, going to my room. "Every time. Every single time. I guess I'm just not meant to kiss him."

"Kiss who?" I heard her yell.

Hey Pac,

I got your letter. *Married?* That one blindsided me, but I understand your reasoning. You have to do what you have to do in this life to make yourself happy. As long as you're smiling, it's all good. I didn't mean your letters lacked substance. You just seemed a little down. Didn't mean to offend you, if I did. I'll be there very soon. I guess you'll be married by the time I get there. Congratulations in advance. I guess. ☺

I read the article you did in *Vibe* magazine again. I just don't understand why no one stepped up to the plate and informed the police or judge or whoever that you weren't even in the room. I mean, if anyone in there was true to you, they would have. I guess I just answered my own statement. They weren't true to you. It's sad sometimes when it takes such drastic circumstances to make us open our eyes and realize who's really there for us and who's not. We tend to be so trusting that, many times, we get sideswiped by the foulest of people, all in the name of trust.

Anyway . . . I can't wait to see you. I'm anxious and ready for the days to pass. I guess it didn't take 4 months after all, huh? How do you feel about this? I don't have any expectations that I can think of. Do you have some? What are they, if you do? I hope our bond in five years will be the kind of bond that friendships should be. We call each other anytime, recognize when we are up or down, and always be there emotionally. Respect, cherish, and teach each other how to be better, more well-rounded people. Just being cool and keeping it real for life, like we said. This is real, and no one will ever be able to take this away from us. Can you feel me?

Don't you dare stop writing me poetry and letters. "Absence makes the heart grow fonder?" Damn my heart growing fonder. It's going to do that anyway. We are not playing games and withholding in order to make me miss you. Real, Pac, real. Besides, I'll starve. Don't starve me. Continue to feed me, as I will you, Boo. The countdown is on!

Forever,
Angela

P.S. Midnight will always be yours. See you tonight. ☺

Chapter 18

THE TRIP

I couldn't sleep. I closed my eyes and took a deep breath. It was 3 A.M. I had only five more hours to go before the plane left.

Five more hours.

It seemed like such a long time ago that I had accepted a bet, and the absurdity of it ran rampant in my mind. I looked across the room and saw the shadows of my luggage against the wall. I couldn't stand the restlessness and got up to get some water. I bumped into Tanya as I was returning to my room.

"You can't sleep either, huh?" I asked, walking to the sliding glass doors and opening them, then we took a seat on the couch.

"Worried?"

"No. Just . . . ready to be there and get all of this buildup over with."

"It'll be all right, Ann."

"I know," I responded. "But if I don't get some sleep, I'm going to look like a monster."

"You'll look fine. You can always sleep on the plane."

"With all this anxiety? Please."

There was a knock on the front door. We both

looked at each other and smiled in the darkness. Rising to my feet, I closed the glass door as Tanya headed to welcome the persistent knocker.

"Looks like I'm not the only one who's not gonna sleep tonight," I said to myself, going into my room and closing the door. I lay across my bed, eyes wide open.

Four more hours.

My alarm went off, and I hit the snooze button. Somewhere along the way, I had finally fallen asleep. I nestled myself back under the covers, and in what seemed like hours, I jumped up disoriented. I remembered why I couldn't sleep in the first place. I knew I had to pick up Tupac's cousin. I looked over at my answering machine, and it wasn't blinking. Which meant his cousin hadn't called. I stood in the middle of the floor, staring at the clock but not seeing the time. My alarm had been set for 4:45 A.M. The clock read 4:51 A.M. It hadn't been hours, just minutes. I wasn't late. I hadn't missed my plane. I was just tripping. My scale was tilted, and I was trying to find some balance. I took a deep breath and sluggishly found my way to the shower. I applied my face, dressed, took a deep breath, picked up my bags, and walked into the living room. It was 5:45 A.M. and I didn't want to wake Tanya, so I left her a note. I was putting my bags in my trunk when I heard the apartment door open. Tanya came out half asleep.

"I didn't want to wake you."

"Have fun," she said sincerely.

"I will. Thanks."

"Call me when you get there and give me a number where you're staying," she said. "And be careful. You do have the emergency number, right?"

"What emergency number?" I asked.

"Nine-one-one! Don't forget it!"

"Yes, Mother."

"You do have extra change for a phone call?"

"Times have changed, Tan. They have things called calling cards now, and I have one. Now get in the house before you wake up all the neighbors and make me late."

I arrived in Decatur, at Thug Mansion, at about 6:30 A.M. Tupac's cousin was waiting, and we headed to the airport. Our plane was due to leave somewhere around 8 A.M., and we arrived at airport parking at 7 A.M. We checked our bags and headed to the gate. It looked like it was going to be a pretty full flight. The sun began to brighten the terminal as I watched the bustling crowd and the workers scurrying about trying to make sure everything was in its proper place. Time seemed to have slowed down, as if I, and everyone around me, was moving in slow motion. Tupac's cousin was talking to me and I was responding, but I didn't know what we were saying. I was aware that we had begun boarding the plane. The ticket agent took my boarding pass, handing me back my stub. I stared at it, then back at her. I saw her lips mouth, "Have a nice flight," and I smiled as I went through the doorway. I turned around and Tupac's cousin was behind me, still sleepy and yawning, but looking like this was just another trip. I'm sure it was for him. We found our seats and buckled in. He closed his eyes almost immediately. Shortly thereafter, we hit the runway.

I loved the way it felt when the plane took off. The speed exhilarated me as my heart pounded faster and faster. While the plane raced up the runway, reality slapped me in the face. *Hard. What are you doing?* rang in my head so loud that I looked around to see if Tupac's cousin had been awakened by the noise. He remained calm, however. *Are you crazy? Have you really thought this out fully?* I thought. The plane began to lift off, and whether or not I truly knew what I was doing, whether or not I was crazy, or whether or not I had thoroughly thought this out was all irrelevant and immaterial. I closed my eyes as we continued to ascend, knowing the reality was that I was on a plane bound for New York and I was going to meet Tupac Amaru Shakur.

I vaguely remember Tupac's cousin asking me if I wanted something to drink. When I opened my eyes again, the plane was flying over New York City. We seemed so close to the buildings, I felt like I could reach out and touch 'em. *What is going on down there?* I thought. The hustle and bustle, the people running here and there, everyone with somewhere to go, somewhere they needed to be. *I must come back and see this place,* I thought to myself. The plane flew over a huge section of buildings, cement and red in color.

"What's that?" I asked Tupac's cousin

"Rikers Island. Pac was there," he said, leaning back in his seat.

"Yeah," I said quietly.

Just a couple of months ago, I had picked up my phone and made a call to this place I was now flying over. A bet had coerced me into writing a letter to a man who had been in this huge mass of cement that I was now flying over. That man had received my letter and made a call to me three days later from inside this structure that I was now flying over. A woman—me—without a clue but with a heart filled with hope, was on her way to see the man who had made the call after receiving the letter and who had been housed inside these walls that I was now flying over.

I felt like the pause button had been pressed on this moment in my life. No one would have thought it would have gone this far. Especially me.

Chapter 19

THE VISIT

The plane eventually landed, and Tupac's cousin and I retrieved our bags and headed for the hotel. After checking in, I changed to a fitted ankle-length dress, and we headed out. The sun was shining as we got into a cab and rode to the ferry that would take us to Clinton Correctional Facility.

This part of New York, about 300 miles north of New York City and near the Canadian border, reminded me of Michigan. There was a faint hint of burnt leaves mixed with something sweet and floral in the air. It was cool outside, but the coolness didn't warrant a jacket.

The ferry pulled up in front of the prison. The prison didn't seem very large from where I stood, but it looked weathered. We walked through a series of checkpoints, and Tupac's cousin signed us in. We waited in a cold cement room filled with file cabinets and old, used office equipment. His cousin sat patiently, while my mind raced a thousand miles a minute. The sun played hide-and-seek behind a wall, then finally shone in unobstructed.

"You're nervous, huh?" his cousin asked, smirking.

I forced a half-smile. "Yeah."

"Just relax. He's cool. You have nothing to worry about," he assured me.

I took a deep breath and stared out the window towards the sun.

We had been sitting in the cement room for what seemed like an eternity when one of the guards finally escorted us to the visiting room. I hesitated as we reached the doorway. Tupac might already be in there, waiting. There was little time to compose myself. I held my breath as we entered, and to my relief, he wasn't there.

The room was medium-size, with four rows of red seats divided by a piece of wood that formed a table. We were the only visitors. I wasn't certain if it was a slow day or if this had been arranged because Tupac was a celebrity. The guard, who sat on a raised platform in the corner, informed us that Tupac would be arriving shortly. "It takes 'em a few to bring him down," he stated matter-of-factly.

Tupac's cousin showed me where the vending machines were across the hall, and I purchased a soft drink and some candy. We returned to the visiting room, and I walked around to the windows, nervous and antsy. I finally sat back down and pretended to be relaxed while sipping my drink. After a while, I heard gates clicking and clanking. I couldn't stand it. Initially, the sounds were off in the distance, but each one got closer and closer. I felt like I was having a slight anxiety attack. There had been so much buildup towards this moment, and now, he was just steps from being in front of me. I jumped up from the table again.

"I'll be back," I told his cousin.

"All right." He laughed.

"It's not funny," I said with a smile, walking towards the door, heading in the direction of the vending machine.

As I reached the hallway, out of my peripheral vision I could see an image in blue bottoms walking with a guard. The image had hair, so as I continued to cross the hall, I told myself it wasn't Tupac because Tupac was bald. I breathed deeply, got a hot chocolate, and started back. I could hear his cousin laughing with someone. I knew it wasn't the guard because the guard wasn't talking, let alone laughing. *Could that figure have been Tupac?* I thought, as my heart began to race again.

Then I heard the familiar laugh. My heart began to beat slow, deep, and hard. It was definitely Tupac. I couldn't move. *C'mon, you've talked to him before,* I told myself. *The letters, the poetry. You're fine. You're familiar. Go in. Now! Go in!*

"Okay. Okay. Okay. It's cool," I whispered to myself. It felt like my feet were stuck in cement.

"Where'd she go?" I heard Tupac ask.

All of a sudden, my feet felt like feathers and I was moving. It was strange. A coolness came over me as I entered the room.

"I'm right here," I said, walking down the aisle, moving closer to Tupac and the chair that I so desperately needed to sit in. There was silence. He was smiling, his cousin was smiling, I was smiling, and if I saw correctly, I believe the guard actually had a smirk on his face.

Tupac and I maintained eye contact. It was definitely him I'd seen in the hallway. He had hair—a lot of hair—and he said he wasn't going to cut it until he was released. He was also thinner than he looked in pictures and on television. But his eyes were big and beautiful, powerful, filled with sensation, filled with the aura that had caught my attention on that interview so long ago. My insides became ignited by his smile. He was high, I realized as I reached my chair, but he was there. I sat down slowly, and neither one of our smiles left our faces.

"Ms. Lovely," he said slowly.

"Tupac," I said, matching his tone.

"You're even more beautiful than in your pictures."

Now I was nervous again. Compliments embarrass me. I smiled. "Thank you," I said shyly. "Finally."

"Finally . . . Are you nervous?" he asked.

"Yes, a little," I responded, lifting my quivering hand before him so that he could see it shake. We laughed. "You?"

"Yeah," he said. We both looked at his cousin, who was amused.

"Whatchu laughin' at?" I said, smiling.

"Ya'll are funny," he said.

"Anyway," Tupac said, bringing those big, pretty eyes back in my direction. "I told Keisha you were coming today, and she was gonna come."

" 'Gonna come?' " I asked hesitantly. "What happened? Why didn't she?"

"She changed her mind."

I exhaled inside. He must have sensed it because he gave me a "I-know-what's-going-on-in-your-head" look.

"What's wrong?" he asked, amused.

"I'm glad she didn't come today. Tomorrow would be cool, but today? I'm nervous enough just meeting you. That would have shocked me if I'd walked in and she was sitting here," I said with a dramatic pause.

"She would have been cool, though."

"I'm sure she would have, but *notice* is cool, too," I said, relieved that she hadn't shown up. I had to get comfortable with him before I could try to ease the knowing jealousy of his Queen. Give me a break.

"She might come tomorrow."

"That's cool, Pac. Tomorrow will be fine."

"Headbanger," he purred, giving me a once-over.

"What?"

"Your dress."

"My roommate thought I should wear something provocative, but I opted not to. I figured you get plenty of that."

"Your roommate had a good thought, but you look good," he laughed. "I would have liked to see more skin," he joked.

"Use your imagination," I said with a laugh. "We know how vivid it can be," I crooned.

He stared at me for what seemed like minutes, saying nothing, smiling a silly smile. He had mentally left the room.

"What are you doing?" I asked.

He said nothing. His cousin laughed, breaking Pac's trance. I looked at the guard, and he shrugged with a smirk. Tupac gave me a full smile. *What did he smoke?* I thought to myself, smiling back at him. "You're retarded," I said to him.

"Ms. Lovely," he said, as if giving the only right answer to a game-show question.

He turned to his cousin and began a conversation with him about happenings with Thug Mansion and the goings-on with certain business ventures and people. I sat there, watching him get serious, then laughing, then getting serious again. His eyebrows accentuated the many expressions his eyes reflected. I was calm. It felt so familiar at this point. The fear had subsided. The anticipation had gone. The nervousness had mellowed. I was sitting in front of Tupac, finally, and his aura was real.

In between the conversations with his cousin and the niceties we exchanged, we held hands, rubbing each other's fingers and palms, each massaging the essence of our emotional high into the hands of the other. We talked about his projects, my photo shoots for my portfolio, our work, our life, and our poetry. He was so different from what I'd pictured all these years. He was not given justice by the media. Granted, he had done some things that warranted the publicity he had received, but right now, at that moment, he was someone I had never seen depicted. I had always thought he just really needed a hug. And before it was all over, I was going to give him one.

Before I realized it, our time was up. Tupac looked at me with those eyes and that smile.

"Can I kiss you?" he asked boyishly.

"Yes."

We both stood. I took a glance at the guard in the corner, as if asking him for permission. Tupac cleared his throat. I smiled.

"You nervous?" he asked.

"I'm as nervous as you are." We both laughed and leaned on the table. I was hesitant. I just knew that something would interrupt this moment. It wouldn't have surprised me if Tanya waltzed through the door just as our eyes closed, or if the guard yelled out *"Stop"* just as we took our last breath, or if his Queen threw her hand between our mouths as our lips began to touch. Something—anything—was going to disrupt this moment. But as the closeness grew and our breaths danced with each other, our eyes locked for that final two seconds, then darkness . . .

Our lips touched. His were so soft and full, forceful but tender. His left hand found its way to the side of my breast, and I let out a small sigh. Our tongues searched each other's mouth with such familiarity and wanting. I opened my eyes once to make sure it was him I was kissing, that I wasn't dreaming, that this moment wasn't an illusion. It was him. Definitely him. I closed my eyes again and lost myself in our moment. I didn't care if his cousin was watching. I didn't care if the guard was mad. And I didn't care, at that moment, that someone who wasn't there would be upset at the sight of this. This was my moment. No, our moment. This was a kiss that engulfed our letters, that wrapped itself around our poetry, that stroked the star we found every night, that held the promises made between two souls, that encompassed the midnight ritual that still lingered in that special place, and that was now swollen with a wanting for more. He moaned, his tongue still probing, but free and content. After what seemed like several minutes, we both started smiling, still kissing, still exploring. Then our lips met again and again and again. Our eyes slowly opened, smiles remaining.

"Damn, Ms. Lovely! Umm umm umm," he whispered softly. "And you taste good."

"You too, Pac. You too," I said, rubbing my hand slowly down his cheek. I could hear the footsteps of the guards. I looked over at the one in the corner, and he smiled. I focused my attention back on Tupac as he said some words to his cousin about tomorrow. He turned to me as his cousin started walking towards the door.

"I'll see you tomorrow," he said softly, leaning in again.

"Okay," I whispered, my words smothered by the fullness of his lips.

"I wish I could have held you so your perfume would be on my shirt," he smiled. "But I guess I'll just have to go back and sniff an envelope." We both laughed. "Bye," he said.

"Bye," I said, watching him leave. He turned around and gave me that electric smile of his as he disappeared through the doorway. I went out into the hall, where his cousin was, and we watched him walk away with the guard. His small frame and his signature walk made me smile as he vanished around a corner. As his cousin and I walked out, I could hear the gates opening and closing behind us in the distance. I wondered how he felt and what he was thinking. I wished he could call me and we could talk about today, but he couldn't. As we reached the air outside the prison walls, I took a deep breath and smiled to myself.

Unbelievable.

That night, two of Tupac's friends came to the hotel to visit with his cousin, and they ordered a pizza and just chilled for a while. They were cool, but I was tired, so I went to bed still overwhelmed by my day. I called my mother and told her how everything had gone, and she was relieved that I was doing okay. I called Tanya and checked in, but told her that I wouldn't tell her anything until I got back home on Sunday. Needless to say, her reaction made it clear that she felt tortured.

The next day, we all went back to Clinton Correctional Facility. It was colder the second day, so I wore a black leather outfit. We sat in the visiting room until they brought Tupac in. He looked a lot higher than he had the day before, but it was all good. He gave his boys love and me a kiss, and sat down across from me.

"Your girl isn't coming?" I said, holding my breath.

"Naw, she didn't want to."

"Did you sleep well?" I asked, smiling, feeling relieved that I would have him to myself again.

"Very well, thanks to you," he smiled.

"You want anything from the vending machine?"

His eyes cascaded over my body and back up to my face. We both smiled. "Headbanger," he crooned. "Yeah, an orange soda."

I looked at the other guys and asked them if they wanted anything, but they were cool. I left the room.

I could hear them talking about music, the industry, business, and home as I re-entered the area. I jumped into the conversation about music, but did more listening than talking. They were trying to come up with ideas for his next album. I had never really been around the music industry, so listening to them create ideas, toss some out, and keep other ones gave me a hint of what goes on. I knew that whenever I heard the next CD, something to do with "boss players" would be in one or more songs. I was there at the conception of an idea for his CD. He was pleased with how well *Me Against the World* was doing and was currently writing songs for the CD he wanted to do upon his release. His boys and his cousin talked among themselves for a little while, giving Tupac and me some somewhat private time. We discussed some of the films he was going to write and talked briefly about the youth center. I filled him in on the stories I was writing. He wanted to read some of them and told me that when he got out, he would help me get a story published. I was excited. I stared at him and thought about how great a guy he was. I felt that he was just misunderstood and so beyond the times. He talked to his boys again, and his ideas seemed to flow effortlessly. Everything seemed like a no-brainer for him. He was a special case, and sitting there, I was blessed—truly. blessed—to have had an opportunity to experience his aura. That's all I could think about as I watched him speak so passionately about his business. Intelligent. Strong. Secure. Able-bodied. Masculine. Take-charge. Nonbullshitter. Sexy.

The time went by so fast. The guys walked out into the hallway as I said my good-byes to Pac.

"You'll come back soon?" he asked.

"Yes. How do you feel now?" I asked, unsure of what I actually expected him to say.

"I feel closer to you because I have the physical to go along with the other things," he said. "How 'bout you?"

"I'm happy that we finally met," I said. "You are an exceptional spirit. This was good."

"Yes, it was," he said, leaning in to kiss me, sliding his hand from my face to my neck, and pulling me into him. The kiss was different this time. It was filled with familiarity, as if he had memorized my movements from yesterday, as if we had kissed hundreds of times. It lasted for a while. We didn't break, and as his lips separated from mine, our faces slid past each other's, and we hugged, lingering, and my body began to swell. As he backed away from the table that separated us, I noticed that his body had swollen, too.

The guard came to get him, and he smiled that smile again.

"I'll call you when I think you're back. You're not gonna stop writing me now, are you?" he asked with a smirk.

"Of course not, and you'd better not either," I warned. We exchanged smiles, and then he was gone.

I gathered up my purse. I could hear his boys saying good-bye as I looked over at the guard in the corner and waved good-bye to him.

Big Syke presented me with a hat before Tupac's cousin and I got on the plane. Other than that, I don't remember too much about the plane ride home, dropping his cousin off at Thug Mansion, or driving myself home. I was dazed by the experience. But I do remember that when I got home that night, Tanya was waiting anxiously for details.

"So, what happened? I want particulars from beginning to end," she said, pouncing on me.

"Let me put my bag in the bedroom, and I'll tell you everything."

Tanya had opened two wine coolers and was waiting for me to sit. She was all smiles. "What did he look like, girl? Like his pictures?" she asked.

"No, he didn't look like his pictures. Just in the face. His hair has grown out, and he was a lot thinner than I thought he would be. But it was still him. Everything about him was Tupac. I just kind of overlooked the ideas I'd had, the photos I'd envisioned, and I saw him."

"Did you kiss him?" she asked, smiling from ear to ear.

"Yes, and it was sooooo good. Slow, deep, and passionate."

I gave her the movements from beginning to end. All the looks, the environment, the conversations, and the vibe of the entire visit on both days. I explained that something had changed on the second day. I couldn't explain it, but something had.

"So, what do you think will happen now?" Tanya asked.

"We will remain friends," I said. "He's going to call me. Probably tomorrow."

"Wow."

"I know. It's surreal, Tan. Simply surreal."

Chapter 20

RELEASE

Pac,

What's up, baby? I enjoyed meeting you and wish we'd had more time together, but I guess there is plenty of time for that. I read about you and Keisha. Congratulations! You need what you need. ☺ My roommate says hello. Anyway, how do you feel now? Has anything changed? I know how we put so much on the unknown that the known just doesn't seem as exciting. Do you feel that? I can't tell. Call me soon. I'll keep this one short. I'll see you at midnight.

Forever,
Angela

Question

(Written exclusively for 2Pac from Angela)

If in the midst of the night
Our stars no longer shine bright
And the corner that lent comforts
Its purpose now somewhat trite

If you're absent what power would be in my twenty strokes
Would looking up at the stars at midnight become a joke
Would the deficiency of our words go missed from within
For which would miss it most, your or my twin?

If I found you outside the gates would you answer with soft phrases
Would you make all your promises truths for these are the
questions my mind raises
In the eye of your storm are there any thoughts of what's to come
Or have the curiosities been appeased and this was all this was to
become

I ask of you Pac to lend me a sign or a short reply
So that I no longer have to ask you questions or simply wonder why?

I had written Tupac several times after I got back, but I didn't receive a response. Maybe it was because he was married. I remember reading an article in *Jet* that said he had failed a urine test on May 25. It went on to say that he had been given sixty days of constant confinement and lost his commissary privileges, which would mean that he didn't have access to envelopes and stamps. Did they take his letters away and he didn't have my address anymore? Did he not write it on his arm this time? Did he not feel me anymore? Was the curiosity settled in his mind? It felt over.

I watched the papers and magazines for his progress and goings-on. He had quite a bit of drama. With all the talk about his possible attack in prison and the conversations surrounding his release and Death Row, I knew that I was the last thing on his mind. I understood. Truly, I did. He was handling his business, so I carried on with mine as the months passed.

Tupac was released in October . . .

"Hello, Ms. Lovely." His voice was playful over the phone.

"Hello!" I smiled. "Man, I thought you had forgotten about me."

"How could I forget about you? I've been caught up in bullshit for the past few months, but I'm out now," he said happily.

"Yes, I've been following you through the media." We both laughed. "I guess they're good for something, huh?"

"Yeah, I guess. So, did I catch you at a bad time?"

"No, not at all. I just finished taking a shower and was just watching some TV."

"Is that right?" he joked.

"That's right," I replied. There was a knock on the door. Tanya was gone, and I wasn't expecting anyone. "Can you hold on for a second?"

"Only for a second," he said playfully.

I looked through the peephole and couldn't quite make out who it was, but he looked familiar.

I opened the door and caught just a glimpse of Tupac in the porch light as he rushed in, pushing me against the wall that was behind me. His mouth engulfed mine. My body felt warm as his tongue retraced the path inside my mouth that he'd discovered months ago. This time was different. Our bodies were able to converge, and his hands found their way inside my robe and began to roam over my body as if they'd been there before. I was a noodle as his mouth found its way to my ears and neck. I couldn't catch my breath as his hands found their way to places that felt like virgin territory.

"Pac," I panted. His mouth came back to mine.

"You always open the door without asking who it is?" he asked, still kissing me and teasing my upper and lower lips.

"What a surprise!" I smiled back, returning the pleasant kisses. "And I thought tonight was going to be boring."

Our tongues found each other again. I slid my hands around

his neck and caressed his bald head, letting out a deep sigh. I closed the door behind him, and we found our way to my bedroom. I laid him on his back and traced his "Thuglife" tattoo with my tongue. His hands found their way into my hair as he pulled my head back and took over. Heavenly. I was blurred, but feelin' lovely . . .

"He's dead!" Tanya rushed into my room. Tupac had been shot and in the hospital for the past few days, and I had zoned out watching the movie *9½ Weeks*.

"What?" I said, startled. "Who's dead?"

"You don't know?" She looked alarmed. "You haven't watched the news today?" she asked, stopping my video and switching the TV to the news.

I shook my head no. I had an awful feeling in the pit of my stomach. His face appeared on the screen, and they showed him speaking. I looked at Tanya questioningly. "He's okay, Tan. Who died?"

Tanya pointed to the TV, and I realized it was an old clip of him. They flashed a photo of Tupac, with "June 16, 1971–September 13, 1996" written on the bottom of it. I couldn't move. I didn't know what to make of it. I had never had anyone I know die. I'd never had anyone I cared about die. It felt like I'd lost something special. This wasn't the way my wonderful story was supposed to end. There were other chapters to be written, other experiences to explore. I felt like the world had lost someone special. I felt for his mom, his family, and everyone who truly loved him. I looked at Tanya, then at the TV.

This wasn't a dream or an illusion. Tupac Amaru Shakur was dead. My experience was over. My hope for him was gone. Reality struck me with a swift punch, and I broke down and cried.

For You

(Written exclusively for Pac for life)

Silence broken by the angst of muted tears
Hearts beating solemn rhythms no one can hear
Time moving in slow motion, no actually it's stopped
It didn't have to come to this. Can you still feel me Tupac?

I'm listening for sound, no a feeling or maybe a word
But you've disappeared from all sight, not a word to be heard
Only the photos, CDs, conversations that linger behind
They say "out of sight out of mind" but that doesn't pertain this
time

The world's at a loss, the impact hitting hard
I asked God why now? Why didn't he pull a different card
Unanswered questions saturate the earth, finding placement in us
all
Who's to blame? Can we point fingers? Who will take the fall?

You said nobody raised you, you were raised in this society
So why did this society breed in you a lifetime of anxiety
Causing the hype, the drama, the misfortune that plagued you
Glorifying the mishaps, waiting to see what you would do

No one stepped up to the plate, to say enough of all that ailed
Society can't look itself in the mirror; truth is they've failed
To guide you to a brighter day to show you there's a better way
Instead they remained mute opting to respond, with nothing to say

Guarded in your heart lack of freedom in your mind
Writing lyrics left and right hoping one day you would find
Somewhere to rest your restless soul of all the things you do

Maybe as fate would have it, God found a place in this world for you
Eternally was your most repeated word, prophesied by words you
spoke
Elements you left behind none of your spirit can be broke
You left behind a part of you for all the world to view
You went out screaming fuck the world, what did they expect from
you?

I close my eyes tormented at the part I played in your life
A girl enthralled by the thug, captured by the portrayal of a man
who already had a wife
But through our letters, our poetry, and the relationship that we
shared
Your realness was felt, honesty appreciated, about you I did care

The world keeps moving in circles, one day passing on to the next
Society mourning the loss of you, trying to rectify, giving respect
It's never too late but unfortunate that it takes something drastic to
realize
What we should have cherished, embraced and embellished; God's
child a definite prize

I hope where you are you're smiling. The smile only you can ignite
In a place filled with peace, harmony and love; no forms of darkness
everything's bright
You deserved some peace and quiet, just sad it had to come to this
Just know that society's sorry for failing you and that you are truly
missed.